THE PHILIPPINES

Text by Lee Buenaventura

Photographs by Joe Cobilla
and The Stock House

MPC

Published by CFW Publications Ltd
1602 Alliance Building
130 Connaught Road Central
Hong Kong

Published in the UK and Europe by
Moorland Publishing Co Ltd
Moor Farm Road, Airfield Estate
Ashbourne, Derbushire
DE6 1HD, England

Printed in Hong Kong

Acknowledgements
I would like to express my gratitude to the Ministry of Tourism of the Republic of the Philippines, to Philippine Airline, and to Daily & Associates of Manila for their generous assistance in the preparation of this book. I am equally indebted to Rafael,Paul, Deanna and Melissa Buenaventura for their unfailing support.

Other titles available in POST GUIDE series:
Australia
Hong Kong
Indonesia
Japan
Malaysia
Singapore
Thailand
Sri Lanka

ISBN 0 86190 210 6

Contents

Introduction

It may not be love at first sight. The glimpse of Manila from an aircraft window reveals a sprawling metropolis of no particular charm. It's more like love at first meeting. The jaded tourist, accustomed to being merely tolerated in much of the world, is at first disbelieving, then astonished, and finally utterly beguiled by the friendly smiles of the Filipino people.

It's a fact that the hospitable Filipinos genuinely like foreigners. They have a particularly warm spot in their hearts for Americans, despite the anti-American rhetoric of some columnists and political aspirants. In the more remote rural areas all Westerners are assumed to be Americans. 'Victory Joe!' calls a grinning youngster to a Dutch tourist, holding fingers aloft in a V-sign.

The obsolete World War II shibboleth amuses, but somehow doesn't startle. Time seems to have passed lightly over the rural Philippines, leaving few changes to mark its passage. Ankle deep in the shimmering waters of a rice paddy, skirt hems looped up under their belts, women in conical hats appear permanently bent at the task of planting rice. A carabao, time-honoured beast of burden, lumbers up out of a mud wallow to plod obediently home behind the small child who tends it.

As evening falls, oil lamps cast flickering shadows on the walls inside small cubicle dwellings. Silhouetted in an open doorway, a guitarist lounges, one foot propped high, strumming a melancholy accompaniment to his song of unrequited love. Two young girls pass by, hurrying homewards, rubber slippers slap-slapping through the dust, their giggles and whispers trailing after them in the darkness. The scene is a timeless moment of rural tranquillity. Suddenly an ear-splitting blast from a transistor radio breaks the spell. It's the 20th century, after all.

Back in Manila it's the 20th century with a vengeance—five-star hotels; high-rise office buildings wrapped in glass; sprawling shopping complexes; the neon glitter of strip joints, discotheques and massage parlours; and everywhere the jarring juxtaposition of poverty and wealth.

On reclaimed land along Manila's scenic Roxas Boulevard, the multi-million dollar Cultural Centre sits in solid splendour above a pool of magnificent splashing fountains. Mercedes-Benz automobiles move slowly up the circular drive, carrying jewel-bedecked matrons to performances by internationally renowned artists. Not far away, bare-bottomed toddlers tumble in the dirt outside makeshift shanties while their mothers scrub clothes on a kerbstone. Manila's aspirations and its realities still have a long way to go before they meet.

Similarly unreconciled are the country's attempts at traffic control and its ever-growing glut of vehicles. Whipping along sweeping boulevards or bouncing over pot-holed back streets, Filipino drivers enjoy the reputation of being possibly the worst in Southeast Asia. Seated behind the wheel, the gracious Filipino metamorphoses into a Grand Prix racer who gives no quarter to those of lesser daring.

But there is much more to the Philippines than big-city *elan* and bucolic peasant scenes. This is a country of multiple and unexpected delights. In the north, antique towns bear the indelible print of Old World Spain, still almost as fresh as yesterday. In the south, shining white mosques, sinuous Moorish art forms and *malong*-draped women proclaim an earlier, different sort of religious invasion.

The lure of off-beat adventure is offered in vast rain forests yet to be explored, majestic volcanoes of deceptive quiescence and watery underworlds of awesome beauty. Scattered in turquoise waters like jewels dropped from the hand of a careless goddess, thousands of uninhabited islands entice the world-weary traveller, their waving palms, sparkling white beaches and coral reefs stirring Robinson Crusoe fantasies.

Not least among the Philippines' fascinations is its people: the macho male who projects a public image of swaggering self-assurance, but expects his wife to carry on where his mother left off; the young matron whose demure manner and fragile beauty mask a hardheaded businesswoman; the wizened, cigar-smoking granny who squats beside her kerbside display of mangoes; the dark-eyed children tending siblings only slightly smaller than themselves.

Their warmth is irresistible. They touch each other frequently—give playful shoves, embrace when they meet, clasp hands as they talk. They hum or sing or tap their feet whenever there is music and often when there is not. They laugh and smile readily, out of amusement, embarrassment, or simple friendliness.

The combination of delightful people, breathtaking scenery, exotic nightlife and lost-paradise beaches makes the Philippines a seductive destination for tourists. True, there are some minor flaws. Gargantuan traffic jams, faltering telephone connections and what appears to be an insouciant disregard for clocks, calendars and time schedules have been known to drive the uninitiated to extremes of temper.

A long-time foreign resident claims to have worked out a foolproof formula for avoiding frustration in matters of time: 'Estimate what seems to be a reasonable time for a thing to happen, multiply it by three and double it again to allow for unforeseen events,' he advises. 'If it takes longer than that, you have a right to start getting annoyed.'

He exaggerates. Yet it must be admitted that the delights of the Philippines are best enjoyed by temporarily setting aside a preoccupation with the merits of brisk efficiency and discovering the pleasure of sauntering, rather than striding, through the day, of marking time by golden sunrises and purple sunsets rather than by the cold hands of a clock. It's a tempo that has served the Philippines well for centuries.

Geography

The Philippines is an island archipelago that begins at 21° latitude, just below Taiwan, and meanders south for more than 1,700 kilometres to a point just four degrees north of the equator, near Borneo. On the west lies the Pacific Ocean, lapping at the coast of the southern islands from the depths of the Mindanao Trench (at 10,675 metres, the second deepest spot on earth). On the east, the relatively shallow waters of the South China Sea stretch away towards Vietnam.

The chain of islands are the peaks of submerged mountain ranges, part of a great submarine cordillera that extends from Japan to Indonesia. The cordillera lies within the well-known 'circle of fire', a volcanic belt bordering the Pacific Ocean.

Geologists believe that land bridges once existed between the islands, as well as extending to Borneo and Sulawesi (Celebes) and possibly Taiwan and the Asian mainland. Paleontologists support the theory. Fossil remains indicate that pygmy elephants, deer, boar, rhinoceros and other land animals once roamed the Philippines.

In prehistoric times volcanic mountains emerged from the ocean floor. Ocean levels rose and fell with the advance and subsequent melting of glaciers. The land bridges disappeared beneath the sea. What remained above the waters are the more than 7,000 islands and islets of the archipelago. Of this number, less than half have been given names and only a tenth are inhabited. The two largest islands of Luzon and Mindanao are home to 60 percent of the republic's 53 million people.

With the exception of a stable region at its southwestern perimeters, the archipelago is extremely mobile, spewing fire from a dozen-odd active volcanoes and periodically shaking citizens from their sleep with heavings of the earth. The islands experience anywhere from nine to sixteen noticeable earthquakes a year, most causing only a slight sensation of vertigo. Quakes of major magnitude occur on the average once every ten years. Even then, most damage and death results from the tsunamis, or giant waves, that follow rather than from the quake itself. The last major earthquake in the Philippines occurred in 1976, when waves crashing 500 metres inland on southern Mindanao dragged entire coastal villages out to sea, leaving 4,000 dead in their wake.

Volcanic eruptions nowadays are deadly only to the imprudent, as these waspish peaks usually signal their intentions well in advance with ominous rumblings and curls of smoke. Among the more famous active volcanoes of the Philippines are Mayon, on the Bicol peninsula, 8,000 feet tall and boasting a near-perfect cone, and fiery little Taal on Luzon, said to be one of the smallest volcanoes in the world. A notable curiosity is tiny Didicas volcano, a half-mile-long chunk of rock which has appeared and disappeared in the northern sea more than once.

THE PHILIPPINES

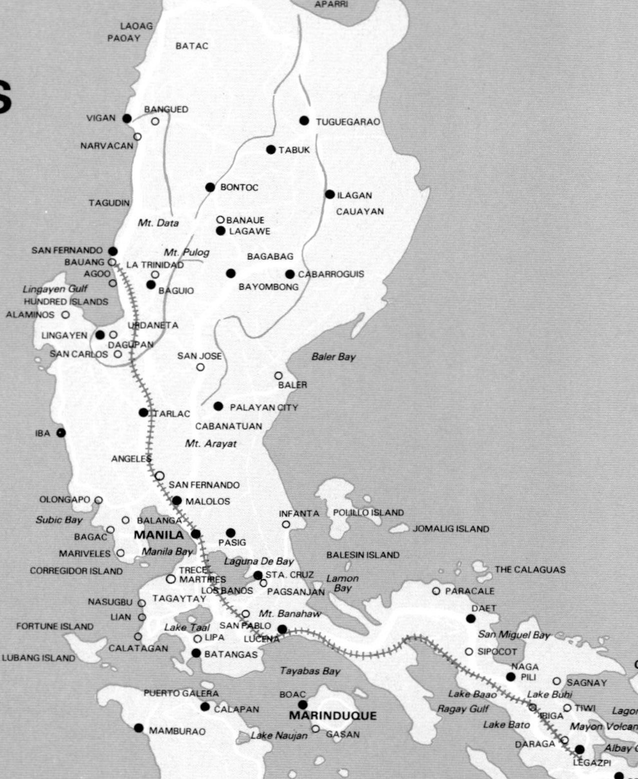

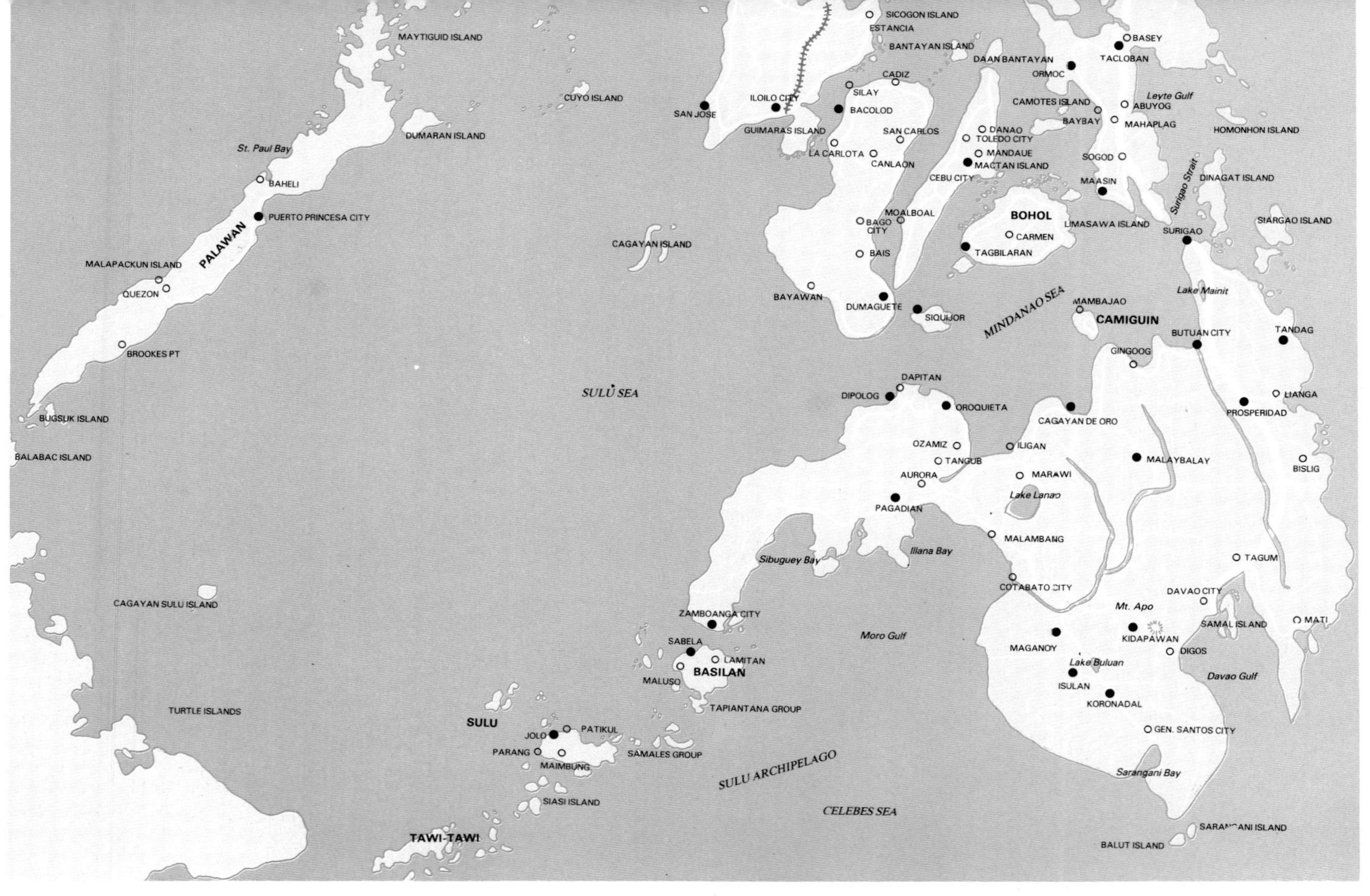
MAYTIGUID ISLAND
CUYO ISLAND
DUMARAN ISLAND
St. Paul Bay
BAHELI
PUERTO PRINCESA CITY
PALAWAN
MALAPACKUN ISLAND
QUEZON
BROOKES PT
BUGSUK ISLAND
BALABAC ISLAND
CAGAYAN ISLAND
SULU SEA
CAGAYAN SULU ISLAND
TURTLE ISLANDS
SAN JOSE
ILOILO CITY
GUIMARAS ISLAND
SICOGON ISLAND
ESTANCIA
BANTAYAN ISLAND
CADIZ
SILAY
BACOLOD
SAN CARLOS
LA CARLOTA
CANLAON
BAGO CITY
MOALBOAL
BAIS
BAYAWAN
DUMAGUETE
SIQUIJOR
DAAN BANTAYAN
ORMOC
CAMOTES ISLAND
DANAO
TOLEDO CITY
MANDAUE
MACTAN ISLAND
CEBU CITY
BOHOL
CARMEN
TAGBILARAN
BASEY
TACLOBAN
Leyte Gulf
ABUYOG
BAYBAY
MAHAPLAG
SOGOD
MAASIN
LIMASAWA ISLAND
HOMONHON ISLAND
Surigao Strait
DINAGAT ISLAND
SIARGAO ISLAND
SURIGAO
Lake Mainit
MINDANAO SEA
MAMBAJAO
CAMIGUIN
BUTUAN CITY
TANDAG
GINGOOG
LIANGA
PROSPERIDAD
DAPITAN
DIPOLOG
OROQUIETA
CAGAYAN DE ORO
OZAMIZ
ILIGAN
TANGUB
MALAYBALAY
BISLIG
AURORA
MARAWI
Lake Lanao
PAGADIAN
MALAMBANG
Illana Bay
Sibuguey Bay
TAGUM
COTABATO CITY
DAVAO CITY
Mt. Apo
MATI
SAMAL ISLAND
KIDAPAWAN
MAGANOY
DIGOS
Lake Buluan
Davao Gulf
ISULAN
KORONADAL
GEN. SANTOS CITY
Sarangani Bay
BALUT ISLAND
ZAMBOANGA CITY
Moro Gulf
SABELA
LAMITAN
MALUSO
BASILAN
TAPIANTANA GROUP
SULU
JOLO
PATIKUL
PARANG
MAIMBUNG
SAMALES GROUP
SULU ARCHIPELAGO
SIASI ISLAND
CELEBES SEA
TAWI-TAWI

The Philippines is usually regarded as having three major island groups. Northern islands are Luzon, site of the nation's capital, and the much smaller Mindoro island. In the middle are the Visayan islands. Mindanao island and the Sulu archipelago lie to the south. The western Palawan island group, although rather isolated, is generally designated as part of 'the south'. For administrative purposes the country is divided into 72 provinces. The smallest units within the provinces are villages, called 'barrios'.

Cascading waterfalls and deep ravines mark the rugged mountains that are the backbones of the large islands. Fertile plains and valleys provide arable land, much of it rich volcanic soil. Natural harbours, small coves and bays, and stretches of white sand beach line the coast.

The vast forests of the country change character with elevation. In the lowland rain forests, giant trees form a dense canopy, preventing sunlight from ever reaching the forest floor, thus leaving it remarkably free of undergrowth and ideal for strolling. At higher elevations are the mossy forests, the 'jungle' of tropical lore, where rare orchids and ferns proliferate and dense undergrowth defies penetration. And in the cool reaches of Mountain province north of Manila, fragrant pine forests scent the air.

The Philippines boasts several rare and unique species of fauna. Some are in danger of extinction, although the Philippine government, in conjunction with international conservation societies, is working to prevent their disappearance. The monkey-eating eagle is now thought to number only a few pairs in Luzon and Mindanao. The tamarao, a horned animal resembling a small water buffalo, is now found only in small numbers in the interior highlands of the island of Mindoro. In a southern Luzon lake swims the microscopic tabios, the world's smallest fish, said to be found nowhere else on earth.

There are other exotic creatures: the tiny mouse deer, a shy, fleet-footed animal barely a foot high; the tarsius, nocturnal and slow-moving, resembling a diminutive monkey with huge, owl-like eyes; the small, curve-beaked sunbird of Palawan, whose brilliant plumage shines with a metallic gleam; jewel-coloured butterflies prized by collectors; and the dreaded king cobra (one of 130 indigenous species of snake).

Offshore, the abundant marine life is a rich source of bounty for seafood lovers, tropical fish fanciers and sea shell collectors. The rare and coveted glory-of-the-seas cone and the leucodon cowrie are found here, as well as many other uncommon varieties, making these waters a Mecca for collectors from all over the world.

History

The Early Filipinos

When the Spanish explorers arrived in the 16th century, they found a well-developed civilisation already flourishing in the Philippines. There was no unified central government, but each settlement, called a *barangay*, had its *datu* who acted as ruler, lawmaker, judge and military commander. Complex religious rites (unless the Muslims had been at work) were performed to placate the capricious spirits of nature. The people composed songs, played musical instruments and wrote a peculiar Indic script.

The early Filipinos' contact with the outside world developed through commerce. Archaeological finds of T'ang dynasty (7th to 9th century) pottery indicate that trade with the Chinese may have flourished even at that early date. In exchange for their pearls, tortoise shell, coral, hemp and gold, Filipinos gained Chinese porcelain, silk, glass beads, lead and iron needles, adding new dimensions to their culture.

A much more potent instrument of change was introduced by Arab traders as they plied Philippine waters on their way from Borneo to south China. Their objective was twofold: commercial enrichment and propagation of the faith. By the time the Spaniards arrived Islam was firmly entrenched in the southern islands, and it remains so up to the present day.

The First Conquistador

Ferdinand Magellan, in search of a westward route to the east and the fabulous Spice Islands, landed in the Philippines in October 1520. On the small island of Limasawa, Magellan paused on Easter Sunday to say mass and proclaim the islands the property of Spain. His proclamation met with no objection from the friendly islanders, who had welcomed the Europeans with food and palm wine and were yet unaware of the portent of the impressive ceremony.

Sailing on to Cebu, Magellan entered into a friendship pact with Rajah Humabon, the local chief. He then held a mass baptism at which Humabon and eight hundred others in attendance were indiscriminately included. The islands were now Spanish and Catholic. It was a moment of triumph in Magellan's life, but from this point on events took a downward turn.

To demonstrate to his newfound Christian brothers the sincerity of his friendship, Magellan ordered all the chieftains of Cebu and neighbouring islands to recognise Humabon as their king. Lapu Lapu, proud chieftain of nearby Mactan island, refused. Magellan went to battle against the recalcitrant chieftain, and in the ghastly fray that ensued the Spaniards fled in disarray, leaving behind their fallen leader.

Rajah Humabon, thoroughly disillusioned by the Spaniards' ineffectual

Villagers washing clothes in a stream

performance, vented his pique by inviting the returning combatants to a feast and attempting to massacre them as they dined. Those who managed to escape eventually returned to King Carlos V with the glad tidings of Spain's new possessions in the East. The stage was set for the colonisation that would begin some forty years later.

The Spanish

Miguel Lopez de Legazpi and his navigator Friar Andres de Urdaneta, who arrived in Cebu in 1565, were the first colonisers of the Philippines. Legazpi professed to prefer diplomacy over force as his tool of persuasion. Whenever diplomatic overtures failed, however, pillage and destruction were the next weapons of choice. Once the native people were subdued, it was given to the friars to bring them into the Christian fold. As Legazpi's expedition moved northwards, this pattern of colonisation continued, the sword and the cross working together for the glory of Spain.

Their explorations eventually brought them to Manila Bay, where they found a Muslim village and fortress located at the mouth of the Pasig River. Recognising the strategic importance of the site, the Spaniards ousted Rajah Soliman, sovereign of the community, and took possession of the settlement that would become Manila, 'Queen of the Orient' in the heady years of the galleon trade.

Bukidnon tribeswomen in colourful head-dresses

At the beginning of the 17th century Spain's dominance was complete. Only the fierce Muslims (dubbed 'Moros' by the Spaniards) and the Igorots of the mountainous interior managed to escape subjugation. Manila had already become the most influential city in the Far East. Each year a galleon destined for Acapulco departed Manila bearing the riches of the Orient—silk, spices, precious stones, perfumes, ornately carved furniture, porcelain—and returned from Mexico carrying silver and churchmen. The Spaniards protected their lucrative position by establishing a trade monopoly that restricted participation to the Philippine governor-general, civil officials and the clergy. The galleon trade thus enriched the coffers of the Spaniards, but retarded economic development of the colony, as virtually all Spanish capital was reinvested in speculation in Chinese goods.

Chinese entrepreneurs flocked to Manila, propelled by hardships in their own country and a keen sense of commerce. They brought to the colony a wide range of essential skills that neither the ruling Spaniards nor the native Filipinos were able to provide. They were tailors, physicians, barbers, locksmiths, merchants. By the time the Spaniards woke up to the fact that the domestic economy was firmly in the hands of the Chinese, it was too late to get rid of the interlopers. Despite restrictions and expulsion orders, uprisings and massacres, the tenacious Chinese remained to intermarry, put down roots and become an integral part of Philippine society.

While the Spanish and Chinese prospered, the lot of the Filipinos was to give their land, their labour and a yearly head tax to the government. Spain, under the *encomienda* system, granted huge parcels of land to religious orders and to Spaniards who had rendered special services to the crown. These grants included not only the land, but the people living on it. Filipinos worked in mines and forests, built ships, constructed buildings and performed personal services for administrators and friars, all under conditions that amounted to slavery.

Outside the city, the clergy were often the only agents of the crown, collecting taxes, supervising labour and dispensing justice. Their prestige and power was enormous, and they guarded it jealously. But there were risks as well as profits in the clergyman's role. Some of the fiercest uprisings were directed against the friars as the only visible government representatives. Particularly odious to the Filipinos was the practice of building a church and forcing the people to build their dwellings around it ('under the bells', as it was termed) so that religious supervision and the collection of tribute could more easily be accomplished. Many of the massive, baroque churches built during the period can still be seen in the central squares of Philippine towns.

In reviewing the record of the Spaniards in the Philippines, it should be borne in mind that the defects of the system were defects of the time. Civil rights, economic and educational opportunity for the masses, separation of church and state, and similar enlightened concepts are products of modern thought. The Spanish colonial system was no worse, and possibly better, than that of some other European nations.

In the 19th century the opening of Manila to foreign trade and the institution of some long overdue reforms allowed a small minority of Filipinos to secure a toehold in the commercial life of the city. Many who did so were *mestizos*, the handsome offspring of Spanish-Filipino unions. They were able to attend school (a privilege previously reserved for Spaniards), learn Spanish and, in some cases, go abroad for higher education. It was among this newly educated class that the seed of nationalism and a passion for reform were born.

The National Hero

Jose Rizal was a physician, novelist, poet, musician, artist, sculptor, historian and philosopher. Above all he was a patriot. While he studied and travelled abroad as a youth, the dismal state of his countrymen was never far from his thoughts. In Spain he joined with other like-minded 'Propagandists' in efforts to prick the conscience of Spain and arouse the indignation of the Filipinos through essays and oratory.

In 1887, at the age of 26, he wrote a novel, *Noli Me Tangere,* that was as much a political statement as a literary work. All the defects of Philippine society were scathingly caricatured—the brutal officials, tyrannical friars, arrogant upper class and obsequious Filipinos. The book was a lighted match to the tinder of seething resentment already grown strong in the Philippines. The people at last had found a voice to express their pent-up bitterness. Although banned by the authorities, copies were widely circulated and Rizal became a hero, uniting the Filipinos in a common urge for reforms.

Still, it was reform, not revolution, that Rizal advocated. He was anti-friar, but not anti-Spain—an intellectual who placed his faith in reason rather than emotion. To the Spanish authorities, however, he was a visible rallying point for the liberationists.

He was arrested, imprisoned in Fort Santiago and on December 30, 1896 executed at the Luneta, now known as Rizal Park. On the eve of his execution he wrote his famous *Ultimo Adios* (Final Farewell), a poem of lyric beauty expressing his love for the Philippines and the Filipinos. Far from extinguishing his light, the Spaniards elevated him to martyrdom in the eyes of his countrymen.

The Revolution

While Rizal, the product of a middle-class educated family, was advocating moderation, Andres Bonifacio, the barely literate son of a poor tailor, was busy propagating a very different doctrine. A voracious reader in spite of his meagre education, Bonifacio pored over books on revolution and developed his own fiery brand of patriotism.

He was instrumental in the formation of the Katipunan, better known as the KKK, a secret society of disillusioned men who busied themselves procuring knives and armaments, increasing their membership and plotting rebellion. The friars, trained to sniff out heresy, were the first to become aware that something was afoot, and nervously communicated their fears to the civil authorities. Lack of evidence, and the cool relations that had developed between the religious orders and the government, hampered investigation.

On August 19, 1896 the unthinkable occurred: one of their own members revealed the Katipunan's activities to the Spanish. Bonifacio and his men fled to the hills of Balintawak, near Manila, where they burned their poll tax receipts as a symbol of the war of liberation about to be launched.

The revolt was premature and destined to failure, as Rizal himself had predicted when he earlier refused an invitation to join the KKK. After months of battle, a truce was drawn up. Emilio Aguinaldo, commander of the revolutionary forces, agreed to voluntary exile in Hong Kong in exchange for a cash settlement and promises of Spanish reforms. Neither side honoured the terms of the truce. Spain worked to consolidate its power in the Philippines while Aguinaldo, in Hong Kong, prepared for future battle.

Umbrellas provide shade

Into this uneasy truce sailed Commodore George Dewey of the United States Navy, to alter irrevocably the course of Philippine history.

The Americans

In 1898 America and Spain were at war. As part of the plan to cripple the Spanish fleet, Commodore Dewey was despatched to the Philippines, where he easily defeated the Spanish in the battle of Manila Bay on May 1. (At one point in the battle Dewey called for a temporary ceasefire to allow his men to enjoy breakfast.)

Emilio Aguinaldo, on hearing of the Spaniards' naval defeat, immediately contacted the Americans and entered into an agreement, the terms of which have been disputed ever since. Aguinaldo claimed that he agreed to help the Americans defeat the Spanish ashore in return for a guarantee of Philippine independence (a promise far exceeding the authority of a commodore, incidentally). Dewey contended that the agreement was simply to unite against a common enemy; no promise of independence was ever given. Historians suggest that in their hasty negotiations, it is possible that neither man was clear on what had actually been concluded.

Whatever the facts about the agreement, the Filipinos and Americans did work together to win the surrender of the Spaniards. Aguinaldo immediately declared the Philippines a republic, with himself as president. American President McKinley, however, announced after intense soul-searching that it was America's duty to take the Filipinos into its care and 'educate, uplift, civilise and Christianise them'. However ignorant McKinley may have been about the Filipinos' cultural and social development, his message was clear. Philippine independence had not yet been won.

The futile rebellion led by Aguinaldo against the Americans was soon put down, and America settled into its avowed task. Schoolteachers and Protestant missionaries arrived, public works were undertaken, roads were built and the framework for a democratic form of government began to take shape. Americans, who treasured their own hard-won independence, disdained the old master-subject tradition of colonial rule. From the beginning they decreed that Filipinos were to be granted the widest possible control over their own affairs. Municipal government was put in the hands of Filipinos, political parties were organised and an assembly composed of elected Filipinos formed the lower house of the legislature. National unity of the archipelago was achieved to a far greater degree than ever before.

American policy had always recognised the inevitability of ultimate self-government, and the Filipinos never ceased agitating for true independence. In 1934 a commonwealth government was established with Manuel L. Quezon as its first president. The plan was to grant independence after ten years of transitional commonwealth rule. World War II intervened.

World War II and Independence

The Japanese appeared over the Philippines on December 8, 1941 a few hours after their attack on Pearl Harbor. Filipino and American forces fought together to repel the Japanese in the weeks that followed, but fell back to the Bataan peninsula, where they endured long months of ceaseless fighting, short rations and few weapons. In May the defending forces capitulated.

Throughout the two years of Japanese occupation, the Filipinos (except for the collaborators, despised by their countrymen) resisted Japanese cajolery to join in the fight for 'Asia for the Asians'. They remained firmly on the side of the West, as they demonstrated in countless acts of personal heroism and unceasing guerilla activity. When General Douglas MacArthur landed in Leyte in October, 1944—fulfilling his famous pledge to the Filipinos, 'I shall return'—Fil-American mutual respect had reached a new high.

On July 4, 1946 Manuel Roxas took office as the first president of the Republic of the Philippines during ceremonies in which full independence was granted. The Filipinos had at last emerged from centuries of subjugation.

Some of its inheritance from its former colonisers was to prove useful to the young nation: a unifying faith, fluency in the language of international relations, a system of mass education, a democratic form of government and proven competence in its administration.

The Philippines Today

The freewheeling democracy the country enjoyed, ended in 1972 when President Marcos declared martial law. But the 1983 assassination of his chief opponent, Senator Benigno Aquino led to his downfall in 1986. In a dramatic and peaceful transition of power that impressed the world, Senator Benigno Aquino's widow, Corazon Aquino, became the Philippines' first woman President.

The new Philippine Constitution assuring the basic rights of Filipinos was ratified in early 1987, signaling the nation's return to democracy. The country is at the moment in the process of political normalisation.

The new government is acknowledged throughout the world and the country remains a member of the United Nations and the Association of South East Asian Nations. And contrary to what might be inferred by news reports, tourists do not put themselves at personal risk by visiting the Philippines.

The People

Each successive wave of foreign migration has left its mark on the features of the Filipino people. The eyes that study the foreiger in frank curiosity may be the large, luminous orbs of the Malay or the narrow, almond eyes of a Chinese forebear. Skin tones vary from deepest tan to the sun-kissed gold of the East-West mix known as *mestizo*.

The imprint of foreign domination is evident in more than physical features. The Filipino has historically displayed an ingenuous eagerness to adopt as his own those aspects of foreign cultures he admires. Thus one finds American slang, Chinese cuisine and Spanish customs firmly embedded in the culture.

But in attitudes and emotions the Filipino is still very much the child of his Malay forefathers. He finds Western straightforwardness shockingly crass, believing the best route to the heart of a matter to be a circuitous one that precludes hurt feelings or loss of face. When his own self-esteem has been injured (and it bruises easily), his gentle nature can revert to a very ungentle thirst for vengeance. He longs for wholehearted approval and is stung by the slightest criticism.

Western pride in independence and self-reliance is regarded with puzzlement by the Filipino, who relies heavily on favours from family and friends to smooth his path through life. Ever conscious of debts of gratitude, he stands ready to reciprocate with whatever resources he has. Civic duty and social conscience are rather foreign to his thinking, however; one's obligation is to one's own circle of family and friends. He is affable and gregarious, happiest when part of a chattering group and distinctly uncomfortable when without a companion. He loves novelty, but fears to innovate and be thought 'different'.

The women of the Philippines deserve special mention. The Filipina's charms are renowned, as she routinely walks off with top honours in international beauty contests and beguiles foreign males with a combination of fragile femininity and intriguing self-assurance. What is not so obvious is the tremendous strength contained in the women of the nation.

It is the wife who holds the purse strings in the Philippines, managing finances with what appears to be inborn business sense. She moves with ease in professional circles commonly considered male domains in other parts of the world. At the lower end of the economic scale, she is often the sole breadwinner for a large brood, going off at dawn to open her small food stall, labour in factories or scrub the floors of the wealthy, returning late at night to tend to the needs of her family. The self-indulgence of the son who marries and fathers children in spite of being unemployed is accepted with equanimity. His sisters will quit school and find work, perhaps as domestic helpers abroad, in order to support him and their ageing parents, buy a needed carabao, or send younger brothers to school.

Possibly nowhere else in the world is education held in such high regard as in the Philippines. Older siblings will go to extraordinary lengths to assist younger ones in obtaining the coveted college degree which they believe will bring economic improvement. In larger cities, eager students can choose among dozens of colleges offering an educational standard that ranges from very good to dismally poor. They study law, business administration, zoology, psychology, unmindful that the few white collar jobs available will go only to graduates of the very best schools. The rest, if they find work at all, may end up running elevators or serving in shops.

Tattooed women of Banaue

Still, it takes a great deal to daunt the exuberant spirit of the Filipino, whose capacity for enjoying life is boundless. '*Bahala na*', he shrugs with optimistic fatalism, 'as God wills', and goes off in search of companions to share a laugh and a meal.

To a foreign observer, the intermittent exhortations of zealous patriots to cast aside foreign influence and search for a true Filipino identity seem unwarranted. The people of the Philippines have indeed undergone cultural blending, but the delightful amalgam that has resulted is unmistakably and uniquely Filipino.

The Ethnic Minorities

There is another Filipino, seldom seen by the tourist who confines his explorations to Manila. The Manileno who attends mass in the morning, eats a hamburger for lunch and gyrates to discotheque music in the evening is a long cultural remove from the four percent ethnic minority population of the country.

Dozens of ethnolinguistic groups are found clustered in the remote highlands and isolated valleys of the archipelago or plying the southern seas. The minorities have traditionally resisted attempts to bring them into the mainstream of Philippine life, with varying degrees of success. Cultural lines continue to blur with increasing exposure to outside influences.

In the past, the greatest influence for change has been the work of religious missionaries. More than half of the ethnic minorities are Muslims. Where Islam failed to make its mark, Christianity has often succeeded. Still, to the despair of orthodox Christians and Muslims, the converts often see no contradiction in continuing to practise ancient animistic rites alongside those of their superficially adopted religions.

Intermarriage with neighbouring tribes, higher education and modern communication all contribute to the ongoing gradual absorption into the common culture. A more ominous instrument of change is the continuing appropriation of tribal lands for various development projects, causing dislocation and accelerating the disintegration of the old cultures.

The few minority groups described here offer only a small sampling of the cultural diversity that exists.

The most interesting to anthropologists, and perhaps the most famous Philippine tribe, is that of the primitive **Tasadays,** who numbered only twenty-six persons when they were discovered living a Stone Age existence in a remote cave of a Mindanao rain forest a few years ago. As a result of their meeting with the outside world, the Tasadays' way of life has already changed, as evidenced by the steel instruments that have replaced their former stone tools.

Scattered throughout the archipelago are the **Negritos** (variously called Aeta, Agta and Ati), a small, dark and kinky-haired people believed to be descendants of the earliest inhabitants of the islands. They are hunters and gatherers who wield spears and bows and arrows with deadly accuracy. Their clothing is bark-cloth and their housing simple lean-to shelters, easily abandoned and constructed anew in keeping with their nomadic lifestyle.

On Luzon island, the northern Cordillera range is home to the Benguet, Ifugao, Bontoc, Kalinga and Apayao, known collectively as **Igorots.** While each tribe's culture is unique, some shared similarities in dress and traditional practices can be found. One of the more unsavoury shared customs of the past was head-hunting raids on neighbouring tribes, culminating in the display of the grisly trophies on posts. These unneighbourly visits were carried out for various reasons, primarily to avenge the death of a kinsman or as a manhood initiation rite, but also to placate peevish gods or satisfy intermittent bloodlust. The practice of head-hunting has long since ceased, but the concept of vengeance murders has not. Rumours of dark doings still filter down to the lowlands.

The traditional basic dress of the Luzon mountain tribes was a wrapped *tapis,* or skirt, for the women and a loincloth for the men. Nowadays only the older women go bare-breasted, and in cool weather the male's G-string is often incongruously topped by a suit jacket.

Tattooing was, and still is to some extent, prevalent among the Igorots as a symbol of social status and prestige, as well as adornment. In Baguio market ancient, cigar-smoking women can still be seen sporting decorative tattoos along the length of their arms. Beads, belts, feathers, flowers and shells are all used to produce items of finery. Among the Kalinga, strings of glass and stone beads are kept within families for generations as treasured heirlooms.

It is the handicrafts of the Cordillera tribes that delight tourists—the beautiful handloomed fabrics, finely crafted woodcarvings of Ifugao deities, and basketware in an incredible variety of sizes and shapes. Travellers who venture into the mountains beyond Baguio will also find fascinating the small settlements of grass-roofed stilt huts tucked picturesquely into folds of the hills.

The shy and timid **Mangyan** live on the island of Mindoro. Notable among the Mangyan tribes are the Hanunoo, who practise a unique method of singing whereby words are sung on the inhaled breath rather than while exhaling, as is usual. They also have retained an ancient system of syllabic writing, apparently of Indic origin, used to inscribe their literature of poetry and folk tales on bamboo cylinders.

Among the Muslim tribes in the south are the **Maranaos** of Lake Lanao on Mindanao island, known equally for their artistry and their quarrelsome nature. The graceful *okir* Islamic folk motif is the common denominator of their exuberant works of art, which include beautiful copper-inlaid brass containers, serpentine woodcarvings and brilliant-hued *malongs,* women's tubular dresses. A less attractive Maranao trait is an extraordinary sensitivity to slights, real or imagined, to personal honour and dignity. The numerous blood feuds engendered are perpetuated down through generations.

Further south are the **Samal,** whose stilt villages dot the coastal waters (and who are the acknowledged masters of Philippine mat weaving), and the **Bajau,** sea gypsies who spend their entire lives aboard their floating homes. Jolo is the home of the **Tausug,** an Islamic group who pride themselves on being formidable warriors. The same fierce aggressiveness that once gave rise to prolonged battles with the Spaniards and Americans is now evidenced in extreme political factions and endless feuds over land ownership.

Among the non-Muslim tribes of Mindanao are the **T'boli,** whose most noted trait is a preoccupation with fashion and beauty. The T'boli woman plucks her eyebrows, powders her face, applies conspicuous beauty spots on the cheeks and carefully styles her hair. Row upon row of brightly coloured beads and brass bracelets adorn her body. Clothing is elaborately embroidered and decked with ornaments. An innate sense of colour and balance somehow manages to tie all these elements together, so that a T'boli woman presents a strikingly beautiful picture, even to Western eyes. The men were formerly as fashion conscious as the women, but alas have succumbed to the jeans and T-shirt costume of the day. T'boli tie-dyed *abaca* cloth is much in demand commercially.

Religion

The vast majority of Filipinos are Christian. Catholicism predominates and plays a central role in the lives of its adherents. Elaborate shrines are standard fixtures in the homes of the wealthy and the intervention of the saints is invoked in times of both major crises (serious illness) and minor anxieties (rainclouds on the day of a garden party). The priest is a necessary adjunct to every important event, intoning blessings over a newlywed couple or a new car with equal solemnity.

Protestant missionaries have made some inroads, particularly in the mountain areas of Luzon. In addition to the conventional Western sects, the Filipinos have contributed some varieties of their own. The most visible is the **Iglesia ni Cristo,** whose needle-spired white churches dot the countryside. The **Aglipayan,** or Philippine Independent Church, formed in 1902 in protest against the Spanish domination of the clergy, now maintains close relations with the Episcopal Church in the United States and the Church of England. Several cults have grown up around national hero Jose Rizal. The most well known is the **Watawat ng Lahim,** which has as its major doctrine the belief that Rizal was a reincarnation of Christ and will enjoy a second coming.

The province of Pangasinan on Luzon island is the centre for the church of the **Espiritistas** who, blending Christian worship with occult practices, have won international fame (or notoriety) as practitioners of psychic surgery and faith healing. Visited by chartered planeloads of believers from abroad, studied by scientists and physicians, the faith healers continue to practise, indifferent to the storm of controversy that surrounds them. While the efficacy of the treatment is inconclusive (medically verified 'cures' and incidences of no improvement at all seem to occur at the hands of the same healer), even the most sceptical witnesses are hard put to explain the phenomena observed in these healing sessions, where eerie things occur in the most commonplace surroundings.

On a small island in the Visayas, Siquijor, nominally Christian shamans practise both white and black magic, complete with the sorcerer's usual paraphernalia, voodoo dolls, skulls and secret rituals. This kind of activity was the despair of the Spanish clergy, whose earnest efforts to eradicate it were obviously not wholly successful. Belief in the powers of the *anting-anting,* or talisman, is common. Outside Quiapo Church in Manila, vendors do a brisk business in amulets bearing a figure of Christ on one side and witchcraft symbols on the other. In the interior mountains, the pagan minorities continue to practise their individual forms of animism, offering animal sacrifices to the spirits of rocks, trees and streams, as they have done for centuries past.

The southern Philippines is the stronghold of Islam, although it too has been adapted to local needs and customs. The religion has been a unifying

Christian-pagan amulets

force in the south but a stumbling block to unity with the rest of the nation, giving rise to separatist movements and continual friction between Muslim and Christian residents.

Language

There are more than 70 languages and dialects spoken in the Philippines. They are part of the Malay-Polynesian language group and share similarities in grammar and sound, but are generally mutually unintelligible. To right this situation a national language, Pilipino, has been developed based on Tagalog, the tongue common to Manila and nearby provinces. When two Filipinos of different linguistic backgrounds meet, however, they will probably converse in English, still the lingua franca of the country decades after the end of American rule.

A minority, usually among the older generation, speaks Spanish, the language of the cultured elite during the 19th century. Because education was the property of the wealthy in Spanish colonial times, the impact of Spanish on the language of the masses was limited to a liberal sprinkling of words, often the names of common objects—*mesa* (table), *ventana* (window), *libro* (book), for example. An exception is Chabacano, a form of pidgin Castilian spoken in Zamboanga. In order to build a fort and establish a community in Zamboanga, the early Spaniards brought in an assembly of

Filipinos from various parts of the country, each speaking a different regional dialect. The Filipinos mixed the Spanish of their overlords with their own native dialects to produce Chabacano.

Influence of earlier cultural associations are also apparent. *Asawa* (spouse) from Sanskrit, *salamat* (thanks) from Arabic and *ate* (elder sister) from the Chinese are a few of the many words of foreign origin found in Tagalog.

Through the Americans' system of mass education, English spread rapidly throughout the country and remained. It is English with a distinctly Filipino flavour, though, and as such it is not always easily understood by other English speakers. The most flawlessly phrased English speech, delivered by a native of Pampanga, complete with clipped vowels, trilled *r*s and transposed *p*s and *f*s, is apt to leave the unattuned listener blank with incomprehension. The wide range of accents among American and British speakers, which often makes communication difficult even among themselves, also presents a problem to Filipino ears. Patience is required on both sides.

Another obstacle to the foreign listener is the Filipino's tendency to lapse into 'Taglish', a merry mixture of English and Tagalog delivered within the bounds of a single sentence. 'Let's stay here *na lang, baka maraming tao* over there,' a Filipino is apt to say. ('Let's just stay here because it's too crowded over there.') Current American slang peppers conversations, and words of questionable refinement are sometimes uttered in very well bred company, apparently having lost their taint of vulgarity in transit.

Certain brand names have become synonymous for the product. All toothpaste is Colgate; refrigerators are Frigidaires; every camera is a Kodak. Some frequently heard expressions and their meanings are: 'blowout'—a celebration treat; 'brownout'—electrical power failure; 'for awhile'—one moment, please; *merienda*—a hearty snack taken between meals; *sige*—okay; *mabuhay*—welcome, good luck, goodbye (a word used as a general toast, conveying best wishes); and *siguro*—literally meaning 'maybe', but in actual practice a courteous way of saying 'no' to a request.

Pilipino (Tagalog) is written phonetically. Pronunciation is similar to Spanish. The visitor might find the following words and expressions useful:

Good morning	*Magandang umaga*
Good afternoon	*Magandang hapon*
Good evening	*Magandang gabi*
How are you?	*Kumusta ka?*
Where is...?	*Saan naroon...?*
Is it far?	*Malayo ba?*
To the right	*Sa kanan*
To the left	*Sa kaliwa*

Straight ahead	*Deretso*
Slow down	*Dahan-dahan*
Stop here	*Dito lang*
Here	*Dito*
There	*Doon*
Wait here	*Magantay ka dito*
Do you have...?	*Mayroon bang...?*
How many?	*Ilan?*
There is none	*Wala*
How much is it?	*Magkano ba?*
How much discount?	*Magkanong tawad?*
Expensive	*Mahal*
Cheaper	*Mas mura*
That's enough	*Tama na*
Just a moment	*Sandali lang*
Why?	*Bakit?*
Hot	*Mainit*
Cold	*Malamig*
Beautiful	*Maganda*
Delicious	*Masarap*
Yes	*Oo (pronounced 'oh-oh')*
No	*Hindi*
Water	*Tubig*
Thank you	*Salamat*
You're welcome	*Walang anuman*

General Information

Climate

Although the visitor will sometimes hear Filipinos speak of a hot season and a cold season, fluctuation of temperature in the Philippines is not extreme. Wet season and dry season are more illuminating terms, as it is the relative humidity that determines whether one basks in the Philippine sun or swelters in it.

Some elevated spots—the cities of Baguio and Tagaytay on Luzon, for example—enjoy mild days and cool nights year round. The rest of the country is generally warmer. In the cities of Manila, Cebu and Davao, the temperature may occasionally rise to highs of 38°C in April and May, the hottest months, but averages about 27°C throughout the rest of the year.

November through March are the pleasantest months, when monsoon winds sweep down from the polar north, bringing dry air and refreshing

Nipa hut and rice paddy

breezes. Lawn parties and golf tournaments proliferate at this time of year.

By April the southwestern monsoon has arrived, carrying heavy, moisture-laden air and creating sultry days and short tempers. Shade umbrellas proliferate on the streets. Folding fans flutter in the hands of wilting female guests at social functions. Those fortunate enough to enjoy such comforts make quick dashes from airconditioned automobiles to airconditioned buildings.

Around June the monsoon rains begin in earnest, bringing relief from the heat. Torrential rainfalls sometimes go on spasmodically for days, flooding streets and highways in low areas. Pedestrians wade through the shallower waters with trousers rolled up and shoes in hand. Enterprising youngsters earn money by ferrying people across the more impassable areas on improvised rafts. After a few days of grey skies, the sun reappears to shine down on freshly washed cities and fields grown green and lush almost overnight.

June to November is also the season of typhoons, those tropical blows that whirl up out of the south Pacific, awesome in size and force. Many dissipate before ever reaching landfall, others have weakened to a mere stiff breeze, and some pass over the islands in full fury, uprooting trees, driving ships up on land and devastating crops. In the aftermath of one of these whoppers, fruit and vegetable prices rise, drinking water is boiled and

Sunset on the water

everyone has a good time trading horror stories about flying tree branches and shattered windows. In the countryside the picture is not so merry. Typhoons take a heavy toll in agricultural crops and livestock. But with the patient resignation born of long experience, the Filipino peasant sweeps aside the debris, replaces the roof on his house and plants his crops once again.

Radio and television stations give typhoon information through a series of signals. Signals I, II and III indicate the approach of a typhoon within 72 hours, 48 hours and 36 hours respectively. At Signal III, it's time to retreat to the safety of a strong building and wait for the passing of the storm and the stretch of sunny, cloudless days which usually follows.

When to Go

December through March are the most pleasant months in terms of weather. April and May are months of sultry heat and humidity in most of the country, made even more uncomfortable by frequent lengthy 'brownouts' (electrical power cuts). Tourist hotels and office buildings generally have their own generators, but shops and restaurants do not. Visitors unaccustomed to tropical weather may find this combination of circumstances trying. On the other hand, some of the most colourful of Philippine fiestas, including the Easter celebrations, occur at this time. Also, the mountain areas of Baguio and Bontoc and the numerous beach resorts provide relief from the heat.

Other months of the year, although sometimes marred by rain or the occasional typhoon, are hot, but not unbearably so. Trade winds and cloud cover contribute to variations in temperature.

Easter and Christmas are when Filipinos travel. Flights are booked weeks or even months ahead. Travel reservations must be made well in advance and reconfirmed upon arrival. Proof of confirmed hotel and flight bookings should be in hand. It's not unheard of for passengers holding confirmed reservations to be 'bumped' from flights due to airline overbooking. Arriving at the airport well before the routine check-in time can prevent this unhappy experience.

Dates of major festival celebrations throughout the Philippines are listed on page 61 under the heading *Fiestas*.

National official holidays are as follows:

New Year's Day	January 1
Holy Thursday	Movable
Good Friday	Movable
Easter Sunday	Movable
Bataan Day	April 9
Labour Day	May 1
Independence Day	June 12
Fil-Am Friendship Day	July 4
National Heroes Day	2nd Sunday in August
All Saints Day	November 1
Bonifacio Day	November 30
Christmas Day	December 25
Jose Rizal Day	December 30

Other holidays may be declared at the president's discretion.

What to Pack

Light cottons and loose-fitting clothes are called for. Synthetics can be uncomfortably warm. Mountain areas may require a sweater or wrap in the evening. So may airconditioned restaurants and theatres.

Daytime wear in the Philippines is extremely casual. Sports shirts, simple dresses, slacks and even jeans seem to go everywhere. Evening wear is a bit more formal, although even then restrictions on dress seldom apply. At the best restaurants and supper clubs and at parties, Philippine women enjoy dressing in glitter and finery.

While business suits and ties may be seen on formal occasions, the most popular dress for men is the *barong tagalog*, a straight-cut shirt worn outside the trousers. The style originated during Spanish times when the Filipinos were not allowed to tuck their shirts inside their trousers, in order to provide a visible distinction (if such were needed) between Spaniard and Filipino. In one of those historical reversals that frequently occur, the Filipinos adopted the style as their national male dress, a symbol of nationalistic pride. The *barong* is a beautiful embroidered garment of lightweight, white or ivory-coloured material. The formal *barong* has long sleeves and is usually made of *jusi*, a fine silk. The short-sleeved variety, called a *polo barong*, may be made of *jusi* or synthetic materials and is used on informal occasions. Ready-to-wear *barongs* are readily available for purchase. Filipinos are always pleased to see foreign visitors wearing the national dress.

On formal occasions the Filipina wears the *terno*. This is a long gown in beautiful colours, featuring huge butterfly sleeves. The dress is cut along simple lines, but elaborately embroidered. The former First Lady, Mrs Marcos often appears in *ternos*, as do Filipina contestants in international beauty contests (which they win with enviable regularity).

Churches no longer require a modest covering of arms, but any excessive display of uncovered flesh will earn glances of reproval. Visitors to mosques must remove their shoes, and female visitors are advised to be well covered.

Raincoats will be uncomfortably hot, but a collapsible umbrella is recommended for protection from both sun and rain. Comfortable walking shoes are, of course, a must. Other items that will contribute to comfort when touring are small, individually wrapped 'wash-up' towels, a plentiful supply of facial tissue, and a folding fan.

Immigration

Visas are not required by tourists staying no more than 21 days, provided they hold valid passports and have visas and tickets for their next port. Exceptions are visitors from countries having no diplomatic relations with the Philippines, stateless persons and nationals of restricted countries.

Longer visits require visas. Persons staying beyond 54 days must register with the Bureau of Immigration. A Temporary Visitor visa issued by a Philippine consular official is good for one year.

Customs

Tourists over the age of eighteen are allowed to bring in the following duty-free goods: 200 cigarettes or 50 cigars or 250 grams of pipe tobacco (in any combination); two standard size bottles of alcoholic beverages; and items for personal use—clothing, perfume, cameras, hairdryers, etc.

At Manila International Airport there are separate Customs inspection lines for passengers having nothing to declare. Tourists are not required to fill out Customs declarations and their luggage usually is not opened for inspection. At most, tourist baggage receives cursory inspection, unless Customs officers have reason to believe dutiable items for other than personal use are being brought into the country.

Prohibited items are the obvious ones; dangerous drugs, narcotics, explosives and firearms, pornographic or seditious materials. The penalty for importation of prohibited drugs (opiates, cocaine, marijuana, hallucinogenics and alpha and beta eucaine) is imprisonment for 14 years to 30 years.

No more than 500 pesos in Philippine currency may be brought into the country. There is no restriction on other currencies, but a currency declaration is required and the amount taken out of the country may not exceed the amount brought in.

Arrival

Most international travellers arrive by air at Manila International Airport. Manila, known as the Gateway to the Orient, is served by both international and regional airlines. Philippine Airlines (PAL), the national carrier, operates between Manila and the United States, Australia, Europe, China, Hong Kong, Tokyo and Southeast Asian capitals. Twenty-three international airlines fly into Manila weekly. Flying time from Hong Kong to Manila is 90 minutes, from Tokyo less than four hours and from Singapore three hours.

The airport, opened in 1982, is attractive, functional and efficient. It is capable of servicing 14 jumbo jets simultaneously and 1,750 passengers per hour. In the baggage claim area is a bank of telephones with direct links to the reservation counters of Metro Manila's leading hotels. Snack bars, banks, information counter, duty-free shop and other conveniences are located in the main complex of the deplaning area. Just outside the Customs area, uniformed authorised porters may be hired. Their fee is three pesos per bag, payable at the porterage desk at the exit.

Major hotels are within 15 to 20 minutes' driving time from the airport. Many hotels will provide free transportation from airport to hotel if arrangements are made ahead of time by telex. Hotel limousines also may be hired upon arrival, but in this case there will be a charge.

Passenger vessels of the following lines call at Manila: Everett Orient Lines, American President Lines and Maritime Company of the Philippines. The passenger terminal, at Pier 7 in South Harbor, has immigration and Customs facilities and is centrally located.

Departure

Tourists leaving from Manila International Airport are subject to an airport tax of 200 pesos, payable in either pesos or any other hard currency.

Emigration Clearance Certificate and a Tax Clearance Certificate.

Philippine currency in excess of 500 pesos may not be taken out of the country. Antiques considered 'cultural properties' (so designated by the National Museum) must have an export permit from the museum. Licensed antique dealers will know which items fall into this category. Items should bear the stamp number of the National Museum.

Inspectors no longer rummage through bags; X-ray machines do the job. Although the machines are considered film-safe, remove film and floppy discs for computers from bags if possible. Recent tests indicate that repeated X-ray exposure does damage these items.

First class lounges of various airlines—Clipper, Marco Polo, Ambassador, Silver Kris, Mabuhay—are located near the gates serving those lines. Restaurants, snack bars and duty free shops are available for departing passengers.

Health

Immunisation certificates are not routinely needed for entry to the Philippines, but may occasionally be required of those arriving from infected areas. Vaccinations are available at the Bureau of Quarantine, 25th Street at South Harbor, Monday through Friday.

Drinking water in Manila is considered safe, but may become contaminated after heavy rains or extended drought. During these periods and when outside Manila, boiled water, soft drinks (without ice) and bottled mineral water is recommended.

Typhoid, malaria and dengue fever are endemic, but not epidemic, in the Philippines. Typhoid may be avoided by eating only peeled fruit and thoroughly cooked vegetables and meat, and by exercising caution in drinking water.

Malaria and dengue fever are both contracted through mosquito bites. Dengue is not life-threatening to healthy adults, but its sobriquet 'breakbone fever' gives some indication of the discomfort it confers. Insect repellents are recommended when sitting out at night or walking through areas of vegetation.

More common hazards are conjunctivitis ('pink eye') and gastrointestinal upsets. Aside from the usual precautions of cleanliness, avoid contact with the eyes when using the small, wet 'wash-up' towels provided by some restaurants and airlines.

Most over-the-counter and prescription medicines are available, often cheaper than elsewhere. Mercury Drug Store, the largest chain, has branches throughout the country. Medical services are very good. Hotels can recommend doctors. A 24-hour emergency service is maintained at Makati Medical Centre, a hospital with modern equipment and facilities, at 2 Amorsolo Street in Makati (Tel. 8159911).

Money

The peso is legal tender. Many merchants will accept US dollars as well. Personal cheques are not usually accepted, but traveller's cheques and credit cards are welcomed in hotels, restaurants and larger shops. Small shops often display a battery of decals indicating the large number of credit cards they accept, but faces fall when a card is actually proffered and the discount you have bargained for will be withdrawn. If your purchase is large enough, however, you may still be able to maintain your bargaining position.

Peso note denominations and their colours are: 100 (purple), 50 (red), 20 (orange), 10 (brown), 5 (green) and 2 (blue). Counting out change requires careful attention because coins of identical denomination, but different form, are in circulation—new, older and oldest. In general, coins grow smaller in size in descending order of value.

Denominations are: two pesos—an eight-sided silver coin; one peso—two silver coins, the large, heavy, older one and a smaller new one; 50 centavos—silver-coloured; 25 centavos—one silver and one brass-coloured; 10 centavos—two silver-coloured coins, the newer one almost weightless; 5 centavos—two brass-coloured coins, one round and one scallop-edged, plus a new silver-coloured coin; and one centavo, small and roughly square.

Foreign currencies may be converted to pesos at authorised foreign exchange dealers. Major hotel cashiers can exchange currencies, but the rate is less favourable than that of banks. All commercial banks are authorised exchange dealers. Banking hours are from 9am to 4pm. Under a scheme devised by the Central Bank of the Philippines, anyone, resident or tourist, who exchanges money at a bank is entitled to one lottery ticket for each US$100 (or equivalent amount in another foreign currency) exchanged. Lottery draws, scrupulously honest, are conducted on the last Thursday of each month and the winner pockets 100,000 pesos, tax free.

As of mid-1988 the Philippine peso was valued at roughly 20 pesos to one US dollar. Exchange rates fluctuate daily and devaluations do occur (twice in 1983). Check the board posted behind counters of bank exchange dealers for current rates of all major currencies.

Tipping

A 10 percent service charge is added to the bill in first-class restaurants and hotels. Any further tip is at the customer's discretion. (Hotel porters are generally given five to ten pesos per bag.) In other establishments 10 percent is usual, perhaps a bit more if the bill is very small. The same is true of barbers and hairdressers. Two or three pesos is sufficient for washroom attendants.

Head waiters, doormen and tour guides do not expect tips. Tipping taxi drivers is not usually done unless large bags or packages are carried, or the

Imee Marcos-Manotoc, daughter of former President and Mrs Marcos.

driver has been unusually helpful in some way.

People outside the service industries who extend small courtesies or assistance to visitors will be embarrassed by offers of money. A warm 'thank you' is all that is required.

Electrical Current

Power supply in Manila is 220 volts AC, 60 cycles. Hotels often have 110 volts capability as well; if not, it is sometimes possible to borrow step-down transformers from hotel housekeeping departments. Power cuts are frequent, but major hotels have their own generators to provide enough current for basic facilities.

Communications

Public telephones are red. Local calls cost 75 centavos; you will need three 25-centavo coins. Shops, restaurants and business establishments will readily offer their private phones for use if a public telephone is not available. Dial 04 for information on directory listings. Some Metro Manila exchanges can be reached quickly; others will draw a constant 'busy' signal, even before dialling is complete. Service is improving as exchanges are upgraded.

Most international calls go through without delay when using direct distance dialling. Operator-assisted overseas calls (dial 08) take longer. Domestic long-distance calls (dial 09) often take longer than international calls.

The Philippine mail service, formerly reputed to be one of the worst in Southeast Asia, has improved considerably in the Metro Manila area. However, cheques and valuables should not be sent through the mail. Money transactions are best handled through bank facilities.

The front desks of hotels will assist with mail and telegrams, or you may go directly to the General Post Office, located at Liwasang Bonifacio. A post office that may be more convenient is located in the Rotary Arcade, next to Tesoro's department store in the Makati Shopping Centre, a popular tourist stop.

Globe-Mackay Cable & Radio Corp.—ITT (Tel. 5213550) at 669 UN Avenue, Ermita has 24-hour service. The main office of the Philippine Telegraph and Telephone Corp. (Tel. 8180511) is at 106 Alvarado Street, Legaspi Village, Makati.

Media

In the earlier times, the Philippine press was one of the most free-wheeling in the world, publishing an outrageous mix of fact and rumour and making little distinction between the two. In the past year, in the face of public demand, newspapers have cautiously moved towards slightly more balanced news coverage.

There are several major dailies in Manila. One of the better English **newspaper** is *Business Day*. The *International Herald Tribune* and *Asian Wall Street Journal* and available at major hotels and news vendors.

International news **magazines** are widely available, as are a variety of other American monthly magazines (at exorbitant prices) and many locally published periodicals.

There are dozens of FM and AM **radio** stations in the Manila area, most broadcasting in both Tagalog and English. FM station DWIM (104.3 mHz) presents hourly news broadcasts in English throughout most of the day.

Five **television** stations operate in Metro Manila. Locally produced programmes are generally in 'Taglish', a mixture of Tagalog and English. They feature variety shows, soap operas, talk shows and sports events. Foreign shows are numerous, mostly American series and movies. The main television news is broadcast in English at 7pm on Channel 4 (the government-owned station), Channel 7 and Channel 9.

Transport

Philippine Airlines (PAL) has regularly scheduled flights to 41 cities throughout the archipelago. Flying times are not lengthy. A direct flight to

Zamboanga, the farthest point from Manila generally visited by tourists, takes one-and-a-half hours. For information on PAL flight schedules, call 8320990. Be sure to take advantage of the special discount fares offered by PAL to visitors to the Philippines. The Thousand Island plan offers 50 percent off all domestic fares to tourists arriving aboard PAL flights from abroad. There are also special fares available to groups, families, students, the elderly, etc.

The Philippine National **Railroad** runs north from Manila as far as Dagupan, Pangasinan (two trains a day, eight hours travel time) and south as far as Legazpi City, near Mayon volcano. The 3pm train to Legazpi City offers airconditioning and sleepers. Trains depart from Tutuban railroad station in the Binondo section of Manila. For information, call 210011 and ask for the ticket office.

For those with plenty of time, inter-island passenger **ships** operate between major island ports. They are not noted for their comfort or convenience. Booking is best done through a travel agent.

Bus travel from Manila to outlying provinces can be quite comfortable. Airconditioning, toilets and even videotaped films are offered on some routes. It also has the advantage of offering views of the 'real' Philippines, splendid rural scenery and small provincial towns. Call Pantranco South (Tel. 874581) or Pantranco North (Tel. 997091). Victory Liner (Tel. 3611506) goes as far north as the mountain resort of Baguio.

Rent-a-car services, with or without a chauffeur, are plentiful. Both Hertz (Tel: 8319827) and Avis (Tel: 8322088) have offices at Manila International Airport and at several major Metro Manila hotels. Unless you are capable of a deft combination of aggressive and defensive driving, you may be better off with a hired driver. If you like a challenge, you will enjoy driving in the Philippines. Traffic moves on the right—usually. You will need a driving licence from your home country or an international licence to drive in the Philippines.

Getting Around in the Cities

For getting around Manila, **taxis** are the most convenient and fastest method (often a good deal faster than one might wish). Asking the driver to slow down is usually futile; closing one's eyes seems to be the best way to avoid anxious moments. Cruising taxis may be hailed anywhere. The amount shown on the meter is the total fare for the trip, not for each individual in the taxi, as the occasional rogue may allege. Unless your destination is a major landmark, a well-known hotel or shopping district, try to get some knowledgeable person—hotel doorman or friend—to explain the route to the taxi driver before you start. Avoid rush hours when normally bad traffic conditions turn abysmal.

Ordinary **buses** go all over the city of Manila. The route is marked on the front of the bus. Special buses, known as the 'Love Bus', ply three fixed routes: Makati–Cubao (Quezon City), Makati–Escolta and Escolta–Cubao. These are airconditioned vehicles which, unlike regular buses, do not accept passengers beyond their seating capacity. There is one fixed fare regardless of distance travelled.

An alternative method of getting about, and one that is much more fun, is by **jeepney.** This vehicle, flamboyant distant cousin of the drab army Jeep, provides more than mere transportation. It offers folk art on wheels. The exterior is a riot of pop-art design. Adorning the hood are silver horses, mirrors and coloured lights. Multicoloured plastic strips flutter from windows and antennae. Painted on the body and on attached wooden signs are names of girlfriends and movie stars, religious slogans, declarations of love and sexual prowess, and pop philosophy. Inside, leis of sweet-smelling sampaguita, the national flower, suspended from the rear-view mirror sway in time with crocheted fringes at the windows. Religious medals and plastic-covered prayers may share space above the windscreen with witty (and often bawdy) sayings. The blaring stereo, formerly standard equipment on jeepneys, has been outlawed recently, but jeepney drivers, a free-spirited, macho lot, do not always feel compelled to comply, so passengers may be treated to the latest in disco hits.

Wandering through the less-travelled streets of old Manila are the *calesas*, horse-drawn **carriages.** They are not allowed on major thoroughfares and are best taken for the novelty of the experience rather than as a means of transportation. Fares to destinations must be negotiated with the drivers, preferably before embarking, to avoid any debate at the end of your journey.

The **Light Rail Transit (LRT)**, an elevated **Metrorail** system, is the most modern and rapid means of transportation in Metro Manila.

In provincial cities and towns outside Manila, there is always plenty of transportation in the form of jeepneys, tricycles, taxis and sometimes fixed-fare taxis. Car hire is available through hotel desks, usually including driver. In more remote areas, jeepneys may be hired for long trips or by the day.

The present economic instability of the country makes it impossible to list fares, as they are constantly changing. It is sufficient to say that public transportation around cities is one of the great bargains in the Philippines, with fares ranging from the equivalent of a few US cents for jeepneys and buses to a few dollars for taxis, depending on distance travelled.

Tours

The traveller with limited time or patience may find the all-inclusive package tour the best way of seeing the country. Philippine Airlines, in co-operation with the Ministry of Tourism, operates PALakbayan tours to all major tourist destinations, which include air fare, hotel, breakfasts and land transportation. Contact the Tourist Information Centre (ask for Tourism Office), Tel: 8322964 or 8321961.

Local tour agencies also offer either standard or individually designed tours. Standard tours offered in the Metro Manila area are half-day and full-day sightseeing of Manila and suburbs, Manila By Night tours which include a visit to the jai alai fronton, special interest museum tours, and tours to Corregidor, Tagaytay and Pagsanjan. Most major hotels either have tour operator offices on the premises or offer their own organised excursions to local attractions. There are hundreds of agents listed in the Yellow Pages of the telephone directory, or Department of Tourism (Tel: 599031 Manila). Listed below are only a few of the best known tour operators and agents:

Acme Tours and Travel Inc. — G/F, Phil Am Building, corner UN Avenue and Orosa Street, Ermita (Tel: 591917 or 588511);

Rajah Tours Philippines — 2nd/F, Royal Bay Terrace, UN Avenue, Ermita (Tel: 596626 or 507849);

Sarkies Tours Philippines — Jose P. Laurel Bldg, corner M H del Pilar and Pedro Gil Streets, Ermita (Tel: 582144 or 572250);

Pan Pacific Travel — 207 Dasmarinas Street, Binindo, Manila (Tel: 479263 or 479269);

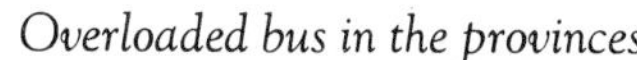

Overloaded bus in the provinces

E C
JACINTO
NOVALICHES
JUN JUN
3
EDGAR
BLUMENTRITT
THE LAWYER No 2
HELLA
HELLA
452 A
PUJ PILIPINAS 80

Satellite Travel — Concessions A&B, Ramona Apartments, 1555 M Adriatico Street, Ermita (Tel: 593920 or 593914).

Where to Stay

For reasons of space, only first-class or luxury class hotels are listed in individual destination sections, where such accommodations are available. These are either of international standard or at least very comfortable. Tariffs are not listed, as the recent devaluation of the peso and the threat of another makes prices rapidly obsolete. A rough estimate of prices in these hotels in Manila would be between US$50 and $75 for a double room, rising to as much as $100 a night in the newer, plushest hotels. In provincial cities, prices drop to a range of $25-$35 for similar accommodation.

Travellers are by no means limited to these hotels. There are many other perfectly acceptable hotels and inns with much lower rates. If you are on a budget, take advantage of the many small pensions and hostels throughout the country, where single rooms go for as little as $6-$10 a night.

If you have not booked accommodations through a travel agent, the best way to learn about the options available to you is through the Department of Tourism, which maintains a complete listing of hotels, inns, etc. and current tariffs. The main office in Manila at Agrafina Circle, Rizal Park (Tel. 599031).

What to Buy

Meticulous craftsmanship, artistic flair and low prices place Philippine handicrafts among the best buys in Asia. Before buying, take the time to compare prices and quality, as both vary widely from one shop to the next.

When shopping at markets or street stalls, you must be prepared to bargain or pay an inflated price. The vendors will not be offended if you haggle; they will be astonished if you don't. Bargaining done in a light, almost playful spirit is fun for both parties to the transaction, the idea being for both to come away thinking they've done well. If you can manage to be the first customer of the day, so much the better. The belief is that a good first sale will impart luck to the whole day's business.

Prices are usually fixed in large department stores, but it's worth asking for a discount anyway, as clerks are sometimes authorised to give as much as ten per cent off to those who ask. Smaller shops and boutiques also claim a 'fixed price' policy, but prices can often be negotiated, especially if the purchase is substantial and payment is in cash.

Duty free shops have an unusual provision here, in that visitors are allowed to buy a limited number of items for use within the country. Each person is entitled to buy two cartons of cigarettes, two bottles of alcohol, perfume and toiletries. You will need to show your passport and onward ticket at the entrance. Purchases may be paid in foreign currency. If you wish to pay in Philippine pesos, any purchase above US$10 will require presentation of your Central Bank currency exchange receipt. Duty free shops in Manila are located at the airport, in the Atrium, 2nd floor, Makati Commercial Centre and in the Manila Hilton, Philippine Plaza and Manila Hotel. Cebu has one duty free shop in the Segura Building on Gorordo Avenue.

All Philippine products are available in Manila, but they are sometimes cheaper in the provinces where they are made. If you plan to travel to one of these provinces, check the prices of their specialities in Manila before going so that you can comparison shop.

Best Buys

Woodcraft—The small town of Paete, about an hour away from Manila, has been famous for its woodcarving for generations. Figurines, trays, bowls, bookends and all manner of objects are carved from fine Philippine hardwoods. The Ifugao of Mountain province (near Baguio) are also justly famous woodcarvers of rice gods, dinnerware and statuary. If you allow plenty of time for browsing, you'll quickly develop an eye for the balanced lines and fine finish that distinguish the better pieces from the crude, carelessly executed wares which are also abundant. Monkeypod, actually the wood of the acacia tree, has an especially beautiful grain. Kamagong, another attractive hardwood darker in colour, is more difficult to work with because of its exceptional hardness, and is generally the more expensive of the two.

Handwoven Fabrics and Embroidery—Handweaving may be a chic pastime in industrialised countries, but in the Philippines it is an integral part of the culture. Minority tribes weave their wrap-around skirts, G-strings and burial blankets in the same way their ancestors have done for generations. Although much of the material now produced is for the commercial market, the same patient skills are used.

Jusi is a fine, lightweight fabric produced by combining silk *abaca* (made from the leaf rib of a banana-like plant) and pineapple fibres. Hand-embroidered lengths of this delicately textured fabric are fashioned into attractive shirts for men (the *barong tagalog*), blouses, dresses and wedding gowns for women, and exquisitely beautiful place-mats and napkins.

Ramie is made from a grass fibre which produces a linen-like material stronger than cotton. It is embroidered by hand or machine and made into table linens.

***Lepanto* cloth** is the name given to the weaving of the mountain tribes near Baguio. Originally utilising bark fibres, the weavers now use a variety of fibres, including synthetics, to make the colourful place-mats, cloth bags, blankets and drapery materials that are favourites with tourists.

A more recent entry to the commercial market is the tie-dyed ***T'nalak***

Basketware for every purpose

cloth of the T'bolis in South Cotabato, Mindanao. Traditionally it had only three colours, the natural beige of the *abaca* from which it was made, and black and red vegetable dyes. Coloured commercial dyes are now used as well. The tapestry-like appearance of the long panels makes them ideal for wall hangings.

Hand-embroidered children's clothes are another good buy at prices unmatched elsewhere.

Baskets—Every conceivable size and shape of basket can be found here. They come from all over the archipelago, bearing their ethnic stamp of origin in the style of weaving and design. The most interesting are those with a utilitarian function—fishermen's traps, locust baskets, grain storage baskets, food carriers, money pouches, back packs and ceremonial baskets. The same range of natural fibres are woven into smart handbags, often found hanging right alongside the baskets.

Brassware—The best brassware is made by the Muslim Maranaos, concentrated mainly around Lake Lanao in northern Mindanao. The Arabic influence is apparent in the hand-engraved geometric designs and graceful shapes of the ornamental pieces. The *naga*, or serpent, and *sari-manok*, a mythical bird, are frequent motifs. Gongs, jewel boxes, miniature cannons and jars and vessels of every size are the more common items. The brass betel box makes an attractive and unusual decorative piece. This is a

set of small boxes contained in a larger one, each of which is used to store one of the ingredients necessary to the social ritual of chewing betel nut.

Sea Shells and Shellcraft—Collectors will be delighted with the variety of shells and the number of shops with this speciality. Cebu City and Zamboanga City are excellent sources of shells. Shells are also used to make jewellery, decorative items and knicknacks. Capiz, a translucent and iridescent shell found in abundance near the shores of the southern Philippine islands, served as window panes in homes in colonial times. It is still extremely popular with decorators aiming for a 'native' look. Chandeliers, lamps, laminated trays, cigarette boxes, jewellery, coasters and chimes are all made from capiz. So is dinnerware and, while it may not be practical for everyday use, a capiz shell bowl filled with ice cream or fruit is a pretty sight indeed.

Shoes and Handbags—Marikina, Rizal, just outside Manila, is the centre of the Philippines' footwear industry. Leather shoes and matching bags in up-to-the-minute styles carry low, low price tags. Quality varies and durability is not always great, but you can't beat the price.

Guitars—Handmade guitars of excellent quality are made in Cebu.

Cigars—World-famous Alhambra and Tabacalera cigars are less expensive here than abroad. If you travel in the provinces, you may catch sight of wizened little old women smoking thin cigars with the lighted end inside their mouths. If you'd like to have a go at it yourself, try La Suerte's Matamis cigars, a popular brand.

Silver—Silver filigree jewellery and ornaments, as delicate in appearance as lacework, and silver spoons of unusual design, come from Baguio.

Furniture—Wicker furniture is well made, well designed and inexpensive. It is also inexpensive to ship, due to its light weight. The best quality comes from Cebu.

Books—If you are travelling through Asia and in search of some light reading, you may be frustrated by the scarcity of English materials and appalled at the prices when you do find them. Not so in the Philippines. A wide and reasonably up-to-date selection of American pocketbooks is available at prices exactly the same as in the US. Some British books, oddly enough, are priced even lower than in their home country.

Antiques—There are some interesting antiques to be had in the Philippines. There is also a thriving industry in fake antiques. With that caveat in mind, antique lovers will enjoy the assortment of oriental ceramics, Philippine furniture, ethnic baskets and carvings, delicately wrought jewellery and combs, hanging lamps and religious art found in the antique shops. Especially popular collectors' items are *santos,* wooden figures of saints. These statues once were the prized adornments of churches and household altars, but their material value seems to have outweighed their spiritual worth and they now gaze down from the dusty shelves of antique shops. *Santos* are especially easy to reproduce and authenticity is difficult to verify. (Also see the note concerning export restrictions on 'cultural properties' in the *Departure* section, page 34.)

Children

Travelling with children is sometimes difficult, but travelling is difficult for children as well. Upset routine, unfamiliar food, sitting for long periods in confined spaces, coping with boredom and constant injunctions to 'behave' are enough to try the temper of any normal child. Fortunately, the scowls and tongue-clicking common to more rigid societies in the face of childish behaviour are absent from the Philippines. Children are showered with love and approval. The cranky crying of a tired child is not considered 'naughty'; neither is youthful exuberance construed as rudeness.

Foreign children, especially those with blonde hair, are the focus of much friendly attention. The compulsion to pat them seems to be irresistible, particularly in the provinces outside Manila. If you don't want your baby touched by strangers, better keep him under wraps. On the other hand, if you're looking for an opportunity to have a friendly conversation with local people, just trot out your fair-haired child.

Touring will be much pleasanter for everyone concerned if children can be excused from those parts of the itinerary that are sure to bore them. Hotels can arrange for competent sitters, and television offers a number of children's programmes and cartoon shows. Naturally there are some activities that will interest both parents and children, the best of which allow the young ones enough freedom of movement to work off excess energy. Hotel swimming pools and beach resorts are obvious choices, but there are other options.

The following are suggestions for the Manila area. All are either in Metro Manila or within driving distance. Detailed information may be found under *Things to See and Do* in the Manila section (page 79), or refer to the Index. Some of the places listed are suitable for very young children; others will be of interest only to the older ones.

Suggested are: the children's playground in Rizal Park, Derham Park playground on Roxas Boulevard, Manila City Zoo and Botanical Garden, the roller skating rink at Luneta Park, Nayong Pilipino Village, Alto Doll Museum, Ayala Museum and bird sanctuary, Barrio San Luis in Intramuros, the Planetarium, Manila City Aquarium, a jeepney factory, a ride on the double-decker sightseeing bus that goes up and down Roxas Boulevard along Manila Bay, a ride in a *calesa*, Fort Santiago, Escudero Coconut Plantation, a trip up Pagsanjan River to the falls.

The fast foods so dear to children's hearts are readily available in Manila. The McDonald's hamburger chain has branches in Greenhills Commercial Centre and in Makati Commercial Centre. Kentucky Fried Chicken seems to be everywhere. Locations are listed in the Yellow Pages of the telephone

ndustries
nc.

directory. The same is true of Shakey's pizza parlours. For more substantial fare, the Jeepney Coffee Shop in the Hotel Inter-Continental has the added attraction of mock-ups of jeepneys which serve as booths. The various *kamayan* restaurants serve native Filipino food, all of which is eaten with the fingers. Children enjoy the novelty of messing about with their hands, and sometimes eat foods they otherwise wouldn't even try. The Kamayan Restaurant is located at 47 Pasay Road, Makati; fifteen minutes south of Manila on the shores of Laguna De Bay Lake is Handaan Sa Bicutan, a *kamayan* restaurant housed in an open-air nipa hut.

Food and Drink

The Filipino's cheerful willingness to absorb and adapt from other cultures is reflected in his cuisine, where Malay, Chinese, Spanish and American influences are all evident. The need to preserve food where refrigeration is a luxury has determined some of the more usual methods of preparation—cured meats, dried fish, viands simmering in vinegar. Economic necessity and the ready availability of certain local ingredients has contributed to a rich variety of regional specialities. Coconut finds its way into almost every dish in the areas where that palm grows. The Ilocano region, where the land is harsh and unyielding, produces goat stew and simple vegetable stews. The Bicol region stands alone in its taste for *sili,* tiny hot chili peppers that set the mouth aflame.

Sugar is plentiful and Filipinos eat lots of it, pouring it into coffee and juices, mixing it with vinegar for a sweet-sour meat dish, and using it in candies, sweet rice cakes and pastries. Rice is the common denominator of all Filipino food, appearing at every meal as an accompaniment or, where income is low, as the main fare.

Restaurant menus are often a mixture of English, Spanish and Tagalog terms. Diners will find it helpful to be able to recognise some of the common Tagalog words describing cooking methods.

Inihaw means broiled or grilled; *ginataan,* simmered in coconut milk; *adobo,* cooked in vinegar and garlic; *paksiw,* stewed in vinegar; *estofado* indicates sugar in the sauce; *kilaw* is not cooked at all, but marinated and eaten raw; *dinuguan* means fresh animal blood is in the dish, giving it a dark black colour; *sinigang* is fish or meat boiled in a sort of sour soup.

A typical Filipino breakfast might include *tapa,* slices of beef or pork that have been marinated in a tasty sauce and then dried, steamed rice, a cup of rich, Spanish-style hot chocolate, sometimes a fried egg and *pan de sal,* small bread rolls.

Main dishes to sample are chicken and pork *adobo, pancit*—a dish of noodles garnished with bits of meat and shrimp—and *kari-kari,* a stew of oxtail and vegetables served in a peanut-flavoured sauce. The *piece de resistance* of any festive occasion is *lechon,* roast suckling pig accompanied by a liver sauce. The crisp, red-brown skin is considered the best part of the *lechon;* the underlying meat is almost an afterthought to the knowledgeable diner. *Lumpia,* comparable to the Chinese spring roll, goes by many names according to what ingredients are tucked inside the wrapper. *Lumpiang ubod* is a special delicacy, a combination of shrimp, ham, vegetables and *ubod,* the heart of young coconut palms. Removing the heart kills the palm, which sounds sinfully decadent but isn't, as the fast-growing plants are cultivated specifically for this purpose.

Fish is abundant. Two of the best are *lapu-lapu,* a grouper, and *bangus,* a bony but very tasty fresh-water milkfish. *Labahita* has a delicate white flesh similar to sole. Any fish that will fit on a platter is served whole. It would be unthinkable to remove the head, where the most flavourful flesh is found. Fish *sinigang* is the bouillabaisse of the Philippines, gathering the freshest fish in the market into an aromatic, slightly tart stew.

Filipinos are more likely to round off their meals with fresh fruit than desserts, reserving the sticky, colourful rice cakes—*puto, bibingka, kuchinta*—and pastries for special occasions. Still, a uniquely Filipino invention that begs to be sampled is *halo-halo.* Sometimes taken as dessert, but more often as a between-meals treat, *halo-halo* is a frosty summer cooler served in a tall glass of crushed ice. The name means mix-mix, an apt description of a concoction of diced fruits, red beans, cubed gelatin, coconut milk, chickpeas, purple yam...the list goes on and on. For special richness, top it off with a scoop of native ice cream—the purple *ube* variety or perhaps the *buco* flavour, made from young coconut.

Tropical fruits abound. Bananas come in dozens of sizes and shapes; mangoes, sweet pineapple and papaya are available all year round. Seasonal fruits, too few and too delicate to have made the journey to foreign lands, offer the pleasure of discovery to visitors. A walk through any open fruit market allows an adventure in tasting; you are expected to sample the smaller fruits before buying.

For the truly adventurous, the Philippines has its share of exotic foods. *Balut,* a fertilised duck egg, is served with beer. To eat it, you crack the end, drink the liquid content, then peel it and eat the embryo. It's a sign of machismo to finish off a *balut* with great gusto. The most famous, or perhaps notorious, fruit of the Philippines is the durian, a large, melon-shaped fruit with an overpowering odour. Those who have sampled its delicious, custard-like flesh are usually willing to forgive its offensive smell. Tart green mango slices, dipped in *bagoong,* a smelly pink sauce of fermented fish or shrimp, is another treat for those who relish robust flavour.

San Miguel beer, made locally, is excellent and so is Philippine rum. A native liquor distilled from the sap of coconut buds is *lambanog.* Proceed with caution. For non-alcoholic refreshment, *calamansi* juice made from a small, green citrus fruit is available everywhere, as is *buco*, a drink of coconut water in which strips of tender young coconut float.

Filipinos eat five times a day, inserting two *meriendas*, or snacks, into the mid-morning and mid-afternoon, so there is never a problem finding a restaurant ready to serve. Although there is no shortage of restaurants serving international food, it's fun to go native at one of the *turo-turo* or *kamayan* restaurants. *Turo-turo* means 'point-point', which is just what you do to make your selection from an array of twenty or more dishes displayed behind a counter. *Kamayan* means 'with the hands', and that is how food is eaten in these restaurants, where baskets lined with banana leaves serve as plates.

Food is much more than simple nourishment to the Filipino; it is a soul-soothing comfort and a pleasure to be shared. The most incidental social meeting will invariably include offerings of food and repeated urgings to take more. Visitors will warm the hearts of their hosts by eating until they are about to burst.

Arts and Entertainment

It sometimes seems to the envious foreigner that a talent for music, dance and the arts is built into the Filipinos' genes, making the arts and

Sili, *hot peppers favoured in Bicol*

entertainment scene in the Philippines one of the liveliest and best in Asia.

An appreciation of the cultural heritage of the nation may be gained through visiting its many museums. Ethnic art, paintings of the masters, historical artefacts and ceramics are all represented. But the best way to understand the East-West blend that is the Philippines today is through its contemporary artists and performers.

To find out what current offerings are, consult the entertainment pages of the local newspapers or the weekly magazine *What's On in Manila,* available in hotels and at newsstands.

The government actively supports the arts, and has built an impressive Cultural Centre complex to that end on Roxas Boulevard in downtown Manila. The main building houses a large concert hall, a small theatre seating 400, a library and an art gallery. A museum is located on the fourth floor and the penthouse floor houses a restaurant. Nearby is the covered open-air Folk Arts Theatre and other buildings designed for exhibitions and conventions. The Cultural Centre has its own resident dance company and 70-member Philharmonic Orchestra. A monthly programme of events may be obtained at the box office.

Art

Early Filipino masters began earning international recognition in the last century. The first of these artists were **Juan Luna** and **Felix Resureccion Hidalgo,** who won prizes at the Madrid Exposition of 1884. Juan Luna dealt with epic themes and heroic subject matter, while Hidalgo found his *metier* in neo-Impressionist seascapes and landscapes. **Fabian de la Rosa,** who depicted ordinary scenes of the Philippines with an intense and immediate sense of reality, won a gold medal at the International Exposition of St Louis in 1904. Later, artists of the classical school such as painter **Fernando Amorsolo** and sculptor **Guillermo Tolentino** earned recognition as leaders in the Philippine art world. In the 40s and 50s the cubist period brought artists like **Cesar Legaspi, Vicente Manansala** and **Fernando Ocampo** to the forefront. The abstractionists emerged in the mid-60s, followed by the avant-garde experimenters.

Today's Philippine art scene is one of creative flurry that defies classification. Whereas artists previously were dependent upon the support of foreign collectors, the past twenty years has seen a tremendous surge of interest in art among Filipinos, providing a nurturing climate for growth and experimentation in the art community. All the major art movements are represented, sometimes more than one in the works of the same artist. If there is a common element in the work of today's artists, it is that the genre subjects of the country provide the touchstone of creation, however diverse the forms of expression.

Many works of the masters of the past are in private collections, but museums and galleries open to the public still offer some of the best representative works for viewing. Living artists whose works are eagerly sought by collectors, and therefore command high prices, are Cesar Legaspi, **Malang, Ang Kiukok, Anita Magsaysay-Ho, Federico Alcuaz** and **Romeo Tabuena,** to name but a few.

Hotels and art galleries are the venues of frequent one-man shows, providing an opportunity to buy the works of up-and-coming artists. And lastly, the Ermita shopping district on Mabini Street in Manila caters to the tourist with carabao/nipa hut paintings by the hundreds at reasonable prices.

Music

Guests at hotels and supper clubs from Tokyo to Singapore are sometimes puzzled to find the entertainment provided by performers with Asian faces and Spanish surnames. These are the modern version of wandering minstrels, the groups who have earned Filipinos the sobriquet 'the musicians of Asia'.

Popular musical trends of the West are eagerly adopted and imitated in the Philippines. A Filipino singer's repertoire is usually a mixture of top-of-the-chart hits from the United States and original Filipino songs with Tagalog lyrics, some of which have earned international awards; *Dahil Sa Iyo* (Because of You) and *Anak* (Child) are two of the loveliest modern Tagalog songs. Top vocalists' shows compare with those of any other country's best. The star is often a young woman whose stunning vocal interpretations belie the absence of formal musical training and sometimes even an inability to read music. The performance is replete with gyrating dancers, back-up singers, shimmering costumes and dazzling lighting effects. **Pilita Corales** and **Nora Aunor** are durable favourites on the pop vocalist scene; **Teresa Carpio** and the beautiful **Kuh Ledesma** are more recent arrivals.

Traditional music of the Philippines—the *kundiman* and *balitaw* (plaintive love songs written in 3/4 time), folk songs, *rondalla* string bands —are sometimes heard at special cultural performances and are available on record as well. The same is true of ethnic music, which survives unsullied by Western influence, played on the brass-gong instruments of the Muslims and the bamboo nose flutes and homemade stringed instruments and drums of the mountain tribes.

The **Bamboo Organ** at Las Pinas Church in Paranaque, Manila, the only one of its kind in the world, is honoured with a week-long festival every February, featuring performances of classical and religious music by Filipino and foreign guest artists. It may be visited at other times as well, when you may request a private mini-performance.

Classical music performances are scheduled regularly in Manila.

Every barrio has its marching band

Philippine artists have distinguished themselves internationally in voice, piano, violin and musical composition. The Cultural Centre of the Philippines on Manila's Roxas Boulevard publishes a monthly bulletin listing presentations by both local and foreign artists and orchestras. Open-air, free concerts are performed by the **Metro Manila Symphony Orchestra** at Rizal Park and other venues around Manila.

Dance

The slender Filipina dancer, her dark eyes and flawless tan skin enhanced by the brilliant hues and ornaments of ethnic dress, moves with graceful agility through the intricate movements of the folk dances. Now she is a haughty Muslim princess, next a flirtatious senorita, then a carefree, laughing field worker. Filipino folk dances reflect the country's diverse cultural influences and the many-sided character of the people. They also demonstrate the Filipino's proclivity for expressing his joys, sorrows, labours, combats and celebrations through dance.

The ***Tinikling,*** danced in imitation of a long-legged field bird, is an especial favourite of visitors, who are often invited to try their skill at escaping entrapment as they hop between two bamboo poles struck together in steadily-increasing rhythm. Other frequently performed dances are: the ***Maglalatik,*** a war dance accompanied by the clack of coconut shells

worn on the dancers' bodies; the ***Pandango Sa Ilaw,*** in which female dancers move gracefully through their steps while balancing lighted oil lamps on their heads and the backs of both hands; and the ***Carinosa,*** a flirtation dance with ladies' fans and gentlemen's handkerchiefs employed in a cat-and-mouse game of courtship.

The **Bayanihan Philippine Dance Company** performs locally—their home base is the Folk Arts Theatre of Manila—and internationally. Other dance troupes periodically present cultural shows around the country, sometimes at restaurants and hotels.

The Philippines also has local dance companies that perform standard classical ballets as well as original ballets with native themes, choreographed by talented Filipinos. Foreign performers of stature are occasionally invited to join the local productions in starring roles.

Theatre

Theatrical arts were introduced by the Spanish. The earliest were the stereotypical dramas known as *Moro-Moro* that depicted the battles between Christians and Muslims—effective instruments of propaganda for the church because the 'good guys' (the Christians) always won. Later, Filipinos proved to the Spaniards how well they had learned their lessons by utilising the *zarzuela,* a popular form of musical stage drama, to spread a little propaganda of their own, directed against their Spanish overlords. These two dramatic forms can be found today in festival pageants and occasional revivals by dramatic groups.

Legitimate modern theatre flourishes in the Philippines today, primarily local productions of Western plays, although Tagalog drama is beginning to be seen. **Repertory Philippines** performs throughout the year in the Insular Life Auditorium in Makati, bringing Manila audiences the latest Broadway hits as well as old standards of the Western theatre. Other drama groups may be seen on a less regular basis at theatres around the city. The Rajah Sulayman Theatre in Fort Santiago is the setting for often innovative productions in both English and Tagalog.

Movies

Foreign films, mainly from the United States, are shown in principal cities of the Philippines, often only a few months after release. Locally-produced Tagalog films are cranked out by the hundred each year. These productions are traditionally either sentimental tear-jerkers, action films saturated with violence, or sexy sizzlers. The latter, known as 'bold' films, have paved the way to fame for many young beauties who then renounce their sinful ways and go on to respectable parts. ('Be sure to see my latest picture. It's the last bold film I'm going to make,' was the come-on delivered by a pretty actress in a recent television promo.)

A new ingredient has begun to appear in local films in recent years—an attempt at quality productions addressing serious themes. Lino Brocka, a talented and respected director, is typical of this new breed of filmmakers. Filipino films have begun to capture awards at international film festivals, and the government sponsors its own annual **Manila Film Festival** to encourage local film companies in upgrading their productions.

To the chagrin of movie house operators, video cassettes of movies are now a big business in the Philippines. For a rental cost of about US$75, private homes and clubs routinely enjoy first-run films from abroad, often before they appear in local downtown theatres.

Fashion Shows

While fashion shows are not usually considered entertainment (nor fashion design art), there is some justification in including the Philippine variety under that heading. Hotel dining rooms regularly become the catwalk for full-scale productions featuring gorgeous, prancing models at lunchtime. These shows draw large audiences made up of Manila's chic upper-class matrons as well as businessmen whose admiring glances are directed less at the garments than at the ladies wearing them. Filipino couturiers stay at the forefront of fashion, and are known for their flair and imagination in the use of colour and fabric, often incorporating Filipino themes with subtle sophistication.

Fiestas

Every year hundreds of fiestas are celebrated in the Philippines. Small wonder, when the fiesta contains so many of the things held dear by Filipinos—convivial fellowship, humour and revelry, drama and colour, piety and passion, plus the opportunity to be both participant and spectator at a terrific show. Annual small-town fiestas also serve to bring sons and daughters back from the big cities to reaffirm the bonds of community so vital to the Filipino.

Overlaid with a Christian veneer, ancient practices of pre-Christian animism persist. Fertility dances and harvest celebrations once offered to spirits in forest clearings are now performed for patron saints under the shadow of church bell towers, the result of the clever Spanish clerics' policy of absorbing what they couldn't eradicate.

Visitors are welcomed with enthusiasm to these extravaganzas of parades, beauty contests, religious processions and street plays. Some of the more well-known and colourful fiestas are:

First Sunday in January—The **Feast of the Three Kings** is celebrated in the towns of Gasan and Santa Cruz in Marinduque. Three costumed men followed by excited throngs of children parade through the towns in a reenactment of the journey of the biblical Magi. (This date marks the official ending of the Christmas celebrations.)

January 9—**Feast of the Black Nazarene** in the Quiapo section of Manila. While the main event takes place in Quiapo, it ultimately ties up rerouted traffic all over Manila. The Black Nazarene is a life-size image of Christ bearing the cross on his shoulder, his suffering countenance streaked with blood from the crown of thorns. The statue, painted black by its unknown sculptor, was brought from Mexico on the Manila galleon. The galleon crew attributed miraculous powers to the Nazarene, as do its present devotees. Dressed in gold-embroidered purple robes, the image is borne through the throngs by barefoot men wearing white T-shirts and sporting white towels around their necks. Other male devotees, similarly garbed, press forward in near hysteria, attempting to touch the statue with their towel, which is then rubbed on the body to cure ailments. Female followers swelter in the sun under heavy maroon robes and wreaths representing the crown of thorns. People clamber on one another's shoulders in their urgent desire to touch the Nazarene, and injuries are not uncommon in the crush.

Third weekend in January—**Sto. Nino de Cebu** in Cebu City is a week-long festival paying homage to the patron saint of Cebu. A 16th century

Houses festooned for Quezon's Pahiyas Festival

Pulilan's Carabao Festival

image of the Sto. Nino, presented to Queen Juana by Magellan, is paraded through the streets to the accompaniment of dancing and celebration. Processions, cultural presentations, fireworks and a carnival atmosphere interspersed with moments of solemnity prevail.

January (movable)—**Ati-Atihan** celebration in Kalibo, Aklan on the island of Panay. This is probably the most well-known fiesta in the Philippines, a Christian-pagan frenzy of revelry akin to the Mardi Gras. Three celebrations are combined in one: commemoration of the friendship pact between native Aetas and newly-arrived Malays in the 13th century; a harvest thanksgiving; and a feast to the patron saint, Sto. Nino. Bodies and faces are daubed with soot, incredible costumes are donned, ranging from fierce warriors to Walt Disney cartoon characters and astronauts, and the revellers dance through the streets for three days to the wild Ati-Atihan rhythm reverberating from drums and church bells. On Sunday morning a bone-weary and hungover crowd throngs to church, where the healing powers of the Sto. Nino are invoked by rubbing the image over arms, legs and backs. Then back to the streets, where the celebration climaxes in a mixed bag procession of stamping and shouting dancers and hymn-singing women counting their rosaries. As this fiesta draws crowds from all over the Philippines, reservations for flights and lodging must be made well in advance.

Late January or early February—**Chinese New Year.** (The date is based on the Chinese lunar calendar. New Year is celebrated on the first day of the first new moon after the sun enters Aquarius. As any astrology buff knows, this occurs some time between January 21 and February 19 on the Gregorian calendar.) Manila's Chinatown erupts into lion dances, open-air Chinese opera performances and prodigious feasting.

February 24-25—**Bale Zamboanga Festival** in Zamboanga City. A two-day celebration participated in by both Christians and Muslims of the region. It features regattas, fairs, indigenous dances and colourful costumes.

March 10-16—**Araw Ng Dabaw** in Davao City. A six-day festival marking the anniversary of the city's founding.

March or April—**Easter** (national). Religious fervour is displayed in solemn ritual, fanatical acts of penitence and joyous celebration during the Easter season. The most riveting of the Easter customs, from a foreign visitor's viewpoint, is that of self-flagellation, common in certain sections of Manila and the seaside towns of Rizal province. On Good Friday, *flagelantes* fulfil penitential vows by trudging the streets, naked to the waist, flogging their backs into bloody stripes with spiked or glass-tipped whips. Others carry their acts of atonement to even more zealous extremes by enduring actual crucifixion for hours (stopping short of the final agony, it should be added). These events always draw a huge crowd of spectators.

In a lighter vein is the **Moriones** celebration of Marinduque island, a folk-religious festival centring upon one Longinus, the name legend has given to the unnamed centurion who pierced Jesus's side with his spear in the biblical account of the crucifixion. Longinus, so the story goes, was blind in one eye until the blood of Jesus spattered on his face and restored his sight. In the Moriones pageant, costumed Roman centurions wearing fierce masks and elaborate Roman headgear march menacingly around town for seven days, playing pranks and otherwise enacting the role of all-round bad guys. On Easter Sunday they engage in riotous pursuit of the newly-converted Longinus, in and out of private houses, around trees and through open fields, accompanied by hordes of shrieking children running alongside. Finally the unfortunate Christian is caught and beheaded, whereupon his one-eyed mask is held aloft to signify his death. Before decapitation, however, Longinus is permitted an impassioned speech in which he affirms his willingness to die as testimony to his faith, thus providing the required upbeat note to an otherwise disheartening climax.

March (movable)—**Baguio Summer Festival.** A week-long series of ethnic dances, parades, music and sports at a time when lowlanders pour into Baguio to escape the heat.

March or April, second Tuesday and Wednesday after Holy Week—**Turumba Festival** in Pakil, Laguna. In pre-Christian days, Pakil's priestesses were noted for their healing ability. Animals were sacrificed, the priestess would mumble incantations over the viscera and then fall into a trance-induced fit of twitching. In an attempt to wean the people from this pagan practice, the Catholic friars transferred their faith from priestesses to the Virgin Mary. Devotees of Pakil's Our Lady of Sorrows now do a peculiar hobbling dance (presumably to denote infirmity) while going through a series of gestures that includes pointing at the image of the Virgin, tapping one another on the face and back and chanting 'Turumba! Turumba!' Participants are undeterred by the fact that the meaning of the word *turumba* and the significance of the gestures are unknown to anyone, including themselves.

March 25—**Sinulog Festival** in Ilog, Negros Occidental. The highlight of this celebration is the *sinulog,* a fertility dance of the Mundos, a primitive tribe of Indonesian origin.

April 24—**Magellan's Landing Celebration** in Cebu City. A fluvial parade, with contests and plays, the main feature being a re-enactment of Magellan's landing. A cross said to be the one planted by Magellan has a starring role.

May—**Santacruzan** is celebrated throughout the country on various dates. It is a pageant commemorating the quest for the true cross by St Helena, mother of Constantine the Great. The prettiest young women of the town, dressed in butterfly-sleeved *ternos,* walk in procession under flower-bedecked canopies.

May—**Flores de Mayo.** Dates vary for this national festival reminiscent of a rites-of-spring celebration. A candlelit procession of flower-bearing women dressed in white go to the churches and offer garlands to the Virgin Mary. Singing and dancing in the churchyard follows.

May 14-15—**Carabao Festival** in Pulilan, Bulacan. The lowly water buffalo ('carabao' in the Philippines) reaches new heights of bovine beauty on this harvest festival dedicated to San Isidro. Scrubbed, shaved and polished, garlanded with flowers and decorated with ribbons, the lumbering beasts are induced to walk on their knees in penitential attitude as they parade by the church. Prizes go to the most beautiful participant.

May 15—**Pahiyas,** the harvest festival in the old towns of Sariaya and Lucban, Quezon. The whole town turns into a rainbow of colour as householders adorn their homes with vegetables, papier-mache life-size dummies dressed as farmers, and the folk-art creation unique to Pahiyas, the *kiping*. The *kiping* are brilliantly tinted rice paste wafers shaped into leaves and arranged with considerable artistry into flamboyant decorations. A procession bearing the image of San Isidro parades through the streets, passing under gift-laden bamboo arches. In the wake of the image there is a scramble to snatch the small gifts from the bamboos.

May 17-19—**Fertility Dance** in Obando, Bulacan. In supplication to San Pascual, Santa Clara and the Virgin of Salambao, childless couples and lovelorn singles dance to a *fandanggo* rhythm in the churchyard and streets, praying to be granted a child or a spouse.

Penitential crucifixion at Easter

June 24—**Feast of San Juan** in San Juan, Metro Manila. The townspeople have their own unique way of honouring John the Baptist, by dousing unwary passers-by with water.

June 24—**Halaran Festival** in Roxas City, Capiz. Tribal dances and festivities in commemoration of the purchase of Panay island by ten Bornean chieftains.

June 28-30—**St Peter and St Paul Celebration** in Apalit, Pampanga, when the images are borne on a raft by fishermen down the Apalit River.

Last Friday in June—**Feast of the Sacred Heart** in Lucban, Quezon. In honour of the Sacred Heart of Jesus, this celebration is also known as the Festival of Giants because of the papier-mache 'giants' paraded through the streets.

First Sunday in July—**Bocaue River Festival** in Bocaue, Bulacan. A miraculous cross (the Holy Cross of Wawa), said to have been found in the Bocaue River by a fisherman 200 years ago, is enshrined in a gaily decorated pagoda on the river for the duration of the festival.

July 29—**Saint Martha River Festival** in Pateros, Metro Manila. Saint Martha, patron saint of Pateros, is honoured with a procession along the Pateros River. A replica of a crocodile follows the barge carrying the image of the saint, who is said to have miraculously interceded to save the town's *balut* (fertilised duck egg) industry from a crafty crocodile many years ago.

August (movable)—**Sumbali** in Bayombong, Nueva Ecija. A week-long festival in honour of Sto. Domingo de Guzman, the highlight of which is the Sumbali dance. Dancers blacken themselves with soot, don G-strings and corn-silk wigs in imitation of the Aetas, an ethnic Negrito group, and perform a war dance.

September 10—**Sunduan** in La Huerta, Paranaque in Metro Manila. Brass bands move from house to house to fetch the eligible young ladies of the town, who emerge dressed in long gowns and carrying parasols. Escorted by formally attired young bachelors, they walk in procession through the town. A reception and luncheon follows at the house of the *hermano mayor* (senior host) of the fiesta.

Third Saturday in September—**Penafrancia** in Naga City, Camarines Sur. One of the more spectacular fluvial processions, in which the image of the Blessed Virgin is transferred to the cathedral and then carried back to Penafrancia Church on a barge down the Naga River. Strangely enough, women are forbidden to take part in this homage to a woman.

September 29—**Ang Sinulog,** or **Michaelmas Day,** in Iligan City, Lanao del Norte. A festival in honour of St Michael the archangel, both saint and folk hero of the Iligans, who credit him with miraculous aid in Christian-Muslim wars of earlier centuries. Elaborately costumed performers depict the battle of St Michael and the dragon; devils, complete with tail and horns, wander about the city, and dancers whirl through the streets to ask or give thanks for favours from the saint.

November 1—**All Saints' Day.** The ancient belief of the pagan Celts that the souls of the dead return to visit their earthly homes on the eve of November 1 evolved into All Saints' Day on the Christian calendar. In the Philippines, the whole nation remembers its dead with a cheerful meeting of the clan in the cemetery. Graves are swept, tombstones scrubbed, flowers, candles, folding chairs and transistor radios are arranged before settling down to the all-day vigil. At mealtimes, picnic baskets emerge and the tombs become buffet tables. Priests move hurriedly through the crowd, scattering holy water on the graves.

Late November—**Grand Canao** in Baguio City. People of the five mountain ethnic groups, commonly lumped together under the umbrella name Igorots, gather for their fiesta known as *canao.* A good opportunity for the visitor to see the collective pageantry of these separate tribes.

December 16—The first of a nine-day series of pre-dawn masses known as the **Misas de Gallo** to mark the opening of the Philippine Christmas season, said to be the longest in the world.

December 24—**Festival of Lanterns** in San Fernando, Pampanga. The star-shaped rice paper lantern, or *farol*, is the symbol of Christmas in the Philippines. San Fernando's Christmas Eve celebration features a parade of multicoloured lanterns that may be as large as 45 feet in diameter, mounted on trucks and lit from within by generators.

December 24—**Panunuluyan** (regional). Mary and Joseph go from house to house in search of lodging, with the whole town participating in the pageant.

Sports

There is plenty of opportunity for the sports enthusiast, whether as spectator or participant, in the Philippines.

Spectator Sports

Basketball, the tall man's sport, draws crowds of frenzied spectators to the Araneta Coliseum in Cubao, Quezon City, where professional teams of the Philippine Basketball Association compete. What they lack in height, the Filipino players make up for in speed and agility, making them the top players in Asia. Every schoolboy fantasises about the day he will sink that winning basket to become the hero of the Philippine sports world, such is the national mania for the game.

In the provinces, the sport that overshadows all others is **cockfighting.** On weekends and holidays the jam-packed cockpit is the venue for bloody contests between combative roosters, their spurs fitted with razor-sharp blades. The gory battle is over in a matter of minutes when the loser either dies or turns tail.

There is one additional requirement to be satisfied; the victor must peck his fallen foe twice. No pecks, no win. To the uninitiated, the groans, shouts and general uproar from the spectators seem to be manifestations of extraordinary bloodthirstiness. In fact the lure of the cockpit is not blood, but money. The feverish excitement witnessed is that of gamblers whose fortunes will rise or fall on the slice of a spur.

The busiest person in the pit is the *kristos,* so named because of the Christ-like stance he maintains, arms raised and outstretched to the side. His job is to remember rapid-fire bids signalled from the crowd, faces of the betters and odds on each fight, which he does with unfailing accuracy and without taking notes of any kind.

Cockpits in the Manila area are the La Loma Cockpit Arena in Quezon City, the Marikina Cockpit and the Paranaque Cockpit.

A game that entices both gamblers and sports enthusiasts is **jai alai,** a variation on handball. The game has its origins in the Basque region of Spain, although earlier versions are said to have been played by the Mayan Indians of Central America.

A hard rubber ball is played off a granite wall at one end of the court, caught by players wearing a cup-shaped basket *(cesta)* laced to the right hand, and delivered again with ferocious speed and power back to the wall. The ball rebounds with velocities up to 150 mph, so a miscalculated move

Igorot men in a tribal festival contest

on the part of a player leaping to receive it can be literally fatal. Players wear helmets to avoid serious injury.

There are two courts, known as *frontons*, in the Philippines, the Manila Fronton on Taft Avenue and another in Cebu City. In addition to spectator seats inside the stadium, the Manila Fronton offers viewing from the airconditioned comfort of the Sky Room Restaurant. Games start at 4pm daily, except Sunday, with 14 games scheduled. Twenty-minute intervals are provided between games for the placing of bets.

Sipa is a popular non-professional ballgame played on school grounds and at the Rizal Court on Rizal Avenue in Manila. It has some similarity to volleyball in that it involves getting a ball over a net, but the ball is made of wicker and the players use only their feet, knees and legs.

Occasionally it is possible to see exhibitions of ***arnis de mano,*** the Philippines' ancient martial art that utilises rattan sticks for thrusting and parrying. Originally a practical skill used in combat, the complicated movements of *arnis de mano* survive now as a sport and have further evolved into the *sinulog* warrior dance spectacles of Samar island.

Manila has two **horseracing** tracks, the Philippine Racing Club at Sta. Ana Race Track and the Manila Jockey Club at San Lazaro Hippodrome. Events are held Wednesdays, Saturdays and Sundays.

Participation Sports

Visitors interested in **keeping fit** might like to jog along with the early risers who congregate at the Cultural Centre complex or at Rizal Park on Roxas Boulevard at about 4am each morning. Early evening runners get together at the Ayala Triangle Park in Makati. For a very small admission fee the track at Rizal Memorial Stadium can be used. The stadium is on Adriatico Street across from Manila's Century Park Sheraton Hotel. The Reed Physical Fitness Centre in the Manila Peninsula Hotel offers short-term memberships to guests who prefer indoor workouts.

Tennis courts in Manila open to the public are found at the Manila Hotel, the Philippine Plaza Hotel, the Philippine Village Hotel and at Rizal Memorial Stadium. Many private clubs have tennis, badminton and pelota courts. (The latter is a racquet-ball game played on an indoor court.) Arrangements to play at clubs may be made through affiliation credentials, invitation by a member, and sometimes through hotel management.

Golfers in Manila may use the public municipal golf course and driving range across from the Manila Hotel in the Rizal Park area. (A mini-golf course is nearby.) Some of the private clubs around Manila boasting excellent courses are Manila Golf and Country Club, Valley Golf Club, Wack Wack Golf and Country Club and Canlubang Golf and Country Club. As with tennis, it is possible to make arrangements to play on these courses with appropriate introductions. There are literally dozens of golf courses around the country, most of them on Luzon. Caddies, carts and golf clubs are available for hire. Further details about golfing can be obtained from the Philippine Tourism Authority's Golf Circuit Division by telephoning 502997.

For **trekkers, hikers** and **mountain climbers,** the Philippines offers opportunities to stroll through virgin forests teeming with wildlife, scale vertical cliffs, stand on the crater rims of volcanoes, explore sacred caves and witness breathtaking panoramas.

Mount Apo, the granddaddy of Philippine mountains at a height of 2,909 metres, is a favourite of climbers. Guides can be arranged at Kidapawan, 112 kms south of Davao City. The trek will take three to four days, passing a small lake with waters alternately boiling hot and icy cold, twin waterfalls, forests of lush ferns and orchids, and climaxing at the peak from which you can peer down into the yellow sulphurous crater of the volcano. April and May are the best months for the climb.

Mount Mayon, near Legazpi, is a living volcano and one of the most exciting mountains to climb. It is also the most perilous, due to the risks of dislodging loose rocks and starting an avalanche, tumbling from the hollow surface peak, being overcome with poisonous fumes, and, of course, the possibility of an eruption. Intrepid climbers, attracted rather than deterred by these risks, scale the mountain regularly. The safest approach is from the northwestern slope at the Mayon Resthouse. Climbers should register at the Volcanology Observatory at the same location. Starting from Legazpi City, allow four days for the trek. The final ascent is a two-hour 40-degree climb over loose cinders and lava sand. Maximum rainfall months are November to January and are not recommended times for the climb.

One hundred and seventy kilometres from Manila, Mt Banahaw, considered a sacred mountain by local residents, teems with legends and superstitions. Guides may be arranged at Santa Lucia, Laguna, through the National Parks and Wildlife Station. The trail passes up a vertical wall, over treacherously slippery boulders, through an extinct crater in the shape of a winding canyon with soaring walls, and finally up a rock formation that offers only surface cracks for handholds. Allow three to four days round trip from Manila. Check local weather conditions before setting out.

A less demanding hike might be to the Batad rice terraces, more impressive than the better-known terraces at Banaue, 20 kms distant. Register with the town mayor of Banaue before setting out for Batad. Another pleasant hike is through the Quezon National Park in Atimonan, Quezon province, a game refuge and bird sanctuary. Trails are well delineated and properly maintained. The hike towards the peak can be accomplished within two hours. There is a picnic and camping site along the route.

The Philippines is a marine paradise for **scuba divers.** Superb coral gardens, dramatic drop-offs, sunken vessels, swarms of tropical reef fish, underwater caves and excellent visibility are the attractions that lure divers from all over the world.

The best known of the diving areas is the Apó Reef in the Mindoro Strait. Batangas, on the southeastern side of Luzon, has developed into a major diving centre, largely due to its easy accessibility from Manila, only two hours away by car. There are many diving resorts here, offering varying degrees of comfort in accommodation. In the Visayas region there are dive areas around Cebu, Mactan island, Negros and Bohol's nearby Cabilao and Panglao islands, among others. The Palawan region offers the excitement of a largely unexplored underwater world.

Scuba trips and equipment rental can be arranged through dive operators in Manila and Cebu.

Some dive operators in Manila are: Aquatropical Sport, Suite 2011, Midtown Hotel Street, Ermita (Tel: 586437); Bonito Island Resort, Dive Centre, 2172-B Pasong Tamo Makati (Tel: 873646); Dive 7000 Resort, Atty Cruz, 2nd/F, Buendia Commercial Centre, Makati (Tel: 8313697); Punta Baluarte, Aqua Sports Concessionarie, Ayala Ave, Makati (Tel: 8162186). In Cebu: Club Pacific, Justice Cabahug Bldg, Gen Maxilom Ave, Cebu City (Tel: 79147); Moalboal Reef Club, PO Box 175, Cebu City (Tel: 54763).

Dive shops which can also arrange for equipment rentals and diving trips are: St Morits Dive Shop, 481-A Flores Street, Manila (Tel. 596126),

Mount Apo's sulphurous crater

with a branch in Cebu City (Tel. 61240); Scuba Centre, 722-D Vito Cruz, Manila (Tel. 594445).

Aquasports lovers and beach loafers alike are referred to the listing of beach resorts below.

Resorts

Beach resorts have proliferated in the Philippines in recent years. The resorts range from the simplest, offering the basic facilities of room, meals, sand and sea, to the cushier sort, referred to in the tourist industry as 'destination resorts', where guests enjoy aquatic sports, golf courses, tennis courts and continental cuisine. Any tour agency can provide current tariff rates and arrange transportation.

Luzon Resorts

Batangas province—The favourite destination of divers. About two-and-a-half hours' drive from Manila.

Dive 7000 Resort
Divemaster-Seafari Philippines
Filipinas International Scuba Haven Resort
Maya-Maya Reef Club

Punta Baluarte Inter-Continental (luxury class: golf course, aquatic sports, horseback riding, tennis, cockfighting)

White Sands Beach Resort

Matabungay Beach Club (aquatic sports, tennis, gymnasium)

Dari-Laut (a floating hotel with luxury accommodations moored between two islands. Especially designed for skin-diving holidays).

Bicol

Kagayonan Sa May Dagat (bowling, tennis, horseback riding, aquatic sports).

Cavite province

Covelandia Island Resort (two swimming pools, tennis courts, mini-golf, boating, bowling)

Puerto Azul Beach Hotel (luxury class: golf course, bowling. About one-and-a-half hours' drive from Manila).

Hundred Islands, Pangasinan province—A cluster of tiny islands, most uninhabited; white sand beaches, skin diving, camping. About five hours by car from Manila. The Philippines Tourism Authority rents luxury houseboats here. Minimum facility hotels in nearby Barrio Lucap.

La Union province—A string of resorts along the South China Sea all with beautiful beaches. About four hours' drive from Manila; one-and-a-half hours from Baguio.

Cresta del Mar Resort and Beach Club

Cresta Ola

Nalinac Beach Resort Hotel

Sun Valley Beach Resort (tennis court, basketball court, diving equipment)

Agoo Plaza (luxury class: olympic size swimming pool; 2 kms of beach).

Quezon province

Balesin Island Resort (golf course, all aquatic sports, hiking and motorcycling. Reached by charter flight, 30 minutes' flying time from Manila's domestic airport)

Tulay Buhangin Island Resort (two-and-a-half hours by car from Manila and ten minutes more by motorboat).

Visayan Islands Resorts

Cebu island and adjacent Mactan island—Primarily water sports. Excellent beaches and accommodations.

Argao Beach Resort (tennis courts, wide variety of water sports equipment)

Sta. Rosa by the Sea (on a tiny coral island reached by boat. Horses, bicycles, boating and diving equipment)

Tambuli Beach Resort

Moalboal Reef Club Dive Resort

Club Pacific Resort Hotel.

Panay island

Sicogon Island Resort (luxury class, tennis, pelota, horseback riding, aquatic sports).

Southern Philippines Resorts

Davao on Mindanao island

Davao Insular Inter-Continental (luxury class: beach, swimming pool, tennis court, putting green and a new casino).

Palawan island

Hyatt Rafols (luxury class: golf course, tennis, pelota, beach, swimming pool).

Metro Manila and Environs

Metro Manila is the heartbeat of the Philippines—the seat of government, centre of education, home of the stars, purveyor of culture and fashion, the smug queen of the nation. To the Manileno, anyone unfortunate enough to live beyond the glamorous city's borders is a *provinciano,* a rustic country cousin.

In 1975, Manila's original perimeters were expanded to include four cities and thirteen municipalities. The resulting metropolis, numbering over seven million inhabitants, was christened Metro Manila. Most tourist attractions are in or near the old City of Manila areas—Ermita, Malate, Intramuros, Binondo, Quiapo—and the newer suburb of Makati.

Destined for greatness by virtue of its magnificent harbour and natural waterway, the Pasig River, the city was already an important trading community when the first Europeans arrived in the 16th century. At that time, the early Filipinos had already given the city its name, Manila being derived from the Tagalog words *may nilad,* referring to the abundance of mangrove growth *(nilad)* flourishing in the then swampy environs.

The Spanish conquistador Miguel Lopez de Legazpi ousted the reigning Muslim chieftain from Maynilad in 1571 and immediately set about building a medieval walled city suitable for habitation by Castilians. Constructed in a roughly triangular shape four kilometres in length, the massive perimeter walls and surrounding moats created a small island of Old World elegance for the upper-class Spaniards who were the only ones allowed within its confines. Intramuros ('within the walls') the city was called, and although most of the original walls are now moss-covered ruins, the district is still known as Intramuros. From here, Spain controlled East-West commerce for centuries, except for a brief interlude in 1762 when the British managed to occupy the city, only to surrender under siege less than two years later.

Slum house in the city

Outside the walls, settlements of Filipinos and Chinese provided the labour and services that allowed the Spanish to enjoy their comfortable way of life. Binondo and Tondo districts, across the Pasig from Intramuros, were home to the Chinese shopkeepers, craftsmen and factory owners. Tondo, historically the breeding ground for 'troublemakers'—rebel leader Andres Bonifacio was born here—maintains its reputation for toughness today and enjoys the dubious honour of being Manila's worst slum district. Binondo was the scene of many bloody Chinese insurrections and massacres in the 17th century, but the tenacious Chinese held fast and the district is still 'Chinatown' to Manila.

Fashionable residential districts Ermita and Malate grew up to the south of Intramuros. Here, gracious mansions housed the emerging middle class Filipinos in the 19th century. Ermita has since metamorphosed into the main tourist district of Manila, a hotchpotch of shops, restaurants, bars and hotels.

The Americans arrived in 1902 to give the names of American states and American statesmen and heroes to Manila's thoroughfares, many of which still remain. The Filipinos not only admired their new rulers, who brought with them the brash, intoxicating confidence of a newly emerging superpower, but were eager to imitate them. Even now, familiar status names—Saks, Bloomingdale's, Fifth Avenue—adorn tiny, hole-in-the-wall shops, billboards proclaim the superiority of American products, and American pop tunes pulsate in the smoky air of the girlie bars.

At the close of World War II Manila lay in smoking ruins, second only to Warsaw in total devastation. But the Filipinos, long accustomed to starting anew in the aftermath of natural disasters such as earthquakes and typhoons, took this horror in stride too. Postwar expansion saw the development of an entire new suburb, Makati, now the business centre of Metro Manila and the site of luxurious subdivisions such as Forbes Park and Dasmarinas, where the wealthy live in splendid isolation from their less fortunate countrymen. As new, more distant modern subdivisions continue to spring up, Manila's centre shifts steadily further away from its birthplace at the mouth of the Pasig.

Because of its multi-faceted heritage, its often incongruous proximity of brassy newness and gracious antiquity, shameless ostentation and distressing shabbiness, Manila defies categorisation. But its very diversity makes it one of the most interesting cities in Asia to explore.

Things to See and Do

Roxas Boulevard

Sweeping along Manila Bay, Roxas Boulevard's tree-lined promenades are favourite spots for strolling lovers and admirers of magnificent sunsets.

Cigar-smoking grandmother

At the boulevard's southern end, a strip of restaurants and popular nightclubs has a rather dispirited look by day, but leaps into lively action at night. Several five-star hotels are located in the same area. Double-decker sightseeing buses operate up and down Roxas Boulevard, and the tourist on his own can hop from one attraction to another along its length by short taxi rides and, in some cases, on foot.

The most impressive structure along the seaward side of the boulevard is the **Cultural Centre of the Philippines,** situated on 52 acres of land reclaimed from the bay. Inaugurated in 1969, the centre provides a physical home for the Filipino arts, including an opera company, symphony orchestra and ballet group. The main gallery, open to visitors from 9am to 6pm every day, has year-round changing exhibits of paintings, sculpture, photography and other art forms. Its three theatres offer the best in local and international performances of music, dance and drama. It also houses a reference library and a small museum. Several other buildings, including the **Folk Arts Theatre, Trade Centre, Convention Centre** and the Philippines Plaza Hotel, share the site.

The Manila Yacht Club is just beside the Cultural Centre complex. By contacting Mr Hermie Admana at the Yacht Club's office (Tel. 502545) arrangements may be made for private rental of sailing or motor craft to cruise Manila Bay.

Across the boulevard from the Cultural Centre is the Central Bank complex. The **Central Bank Money Museum** (open 10am-5pm except Mondays) is located here, as well as the **Metropolitan Museum** (open 9am-6pm Tuesday to Saturday; 9am-1pm Sunday). The Metropolitan's permanent collection of art is small, but borrowed works of high quality are frequently exhibited. In the same general area at 10 Lancaster Avenue, behind the Hyatt Regency Hotel, is the **Lopez Memorial Museum** (open 7.30am-noon, 1-4.30pm daily except Sunday), housing a fine collection of paintings by early Filipino masters, rare books and archaeological artefacts.

In the block behind the Central Bank complex at M. Adriatico Street is the **Manila Zoo and Botanical Gardens,** which includes picnic areas and playgrounds. The exotic animals indigenous to the Philippines may be seen here, along with the usual assortment of wild animals and birds. (Open daily 7am-6pm.)

Moving north along the boulevard, one passes the US Embassy and, just beside it, the **Museum of Philippine Arts** (open 9am-6pm daily except Monday).

Rizal Park

Just after the Museum of Philippine Arts, the Quirino Grandstand on the left and the **Jose Rizal National Monument** on the right side of the boulevard mark the entrance to **Rizal National Park.** The park is an oasis of gardens, lagoons, fountains and playgrounds. There are Chinese,

Japanese and Italian gardens, a skating rink, children's playground and a huge grassy topographical map of the Philippines complete with surrounding waters.

On the north side of the park is the **Manila Planetarium** (open daily from 10.30am to 1.30pm and from 3.30pm to 6pm). The **National Library** is within the park, and at its easternmost end are the Ministry of Tourism building and the old Congress of the Philippines, where the **National Museum** is housed (open 9am to noon, 2-5pm daily). The museum has exhibits depicting the culture, history and geography of the Philippines.

Quirino Grandstand, at the park's western limit along the bay, is often the venue of open-air concerts and other entertainment programmes, with free admission. Behind the grandstand, a public ferry operates on weekends and holidays, offering sightseeing cruises around the bay.

North from the Quirino Grandstand, overlooking the harbour, is the **Manila Hotel.** Hotels are generally not considered tourist attractions, but the Manila Hotel, besides being one of the loveliest in Asia, is rich in history. General Douglas MacArthur made his home in the penthouse before World War II, and in the final days of the war the hotel was wrested from the occupying Japanese troops in a room-by-room battle. Over the years since its opening in 1912, the most important social events routinely have been held here. Recent reconstruction and renovation not only managed to preserve the original facade, but produced a lobby that is a showpiece of Philippine materials and craftsmanship.

Intramuros

At the northern end of Roxas Boulevard lies the old walled city of **Intramuros**. The moat which once surrounded the city was filled in during the American regime—they felt it constituted a health hazard—and is now a 17-hole municipal golf course. The walls themselves are largely a memory, but some restoration has taken place, notably some of the magnificent gates which were opened at sunrise and closed at sunset.

Intramuros had already deteriorated into a shabby ghost of its former self before the savage Battle of Manila completely devastated it in 1945. Postwar years saw the ancient city given over to squatters and ugly warehouses. One of the most ambitious ongoing projects undertaken by the government is the restoration of Intramuros. **Casa Manila,** across the street from St Augustine Church, is one of three structures that are authentic reproductions of 19th century houses. The mellow atmosphere of opulence and luxury enjoyed by wealthy families of that era is brought to life in the antique furnishings of Casa Manila and its lovely courtyard with central fountain. The two other buildings contain shops selling antiques and handicrafts and a coffee shop (open 9am-noon, 1-6pm daily except Monday).

At the mouth of the Pasig River, on the same spot where Chief

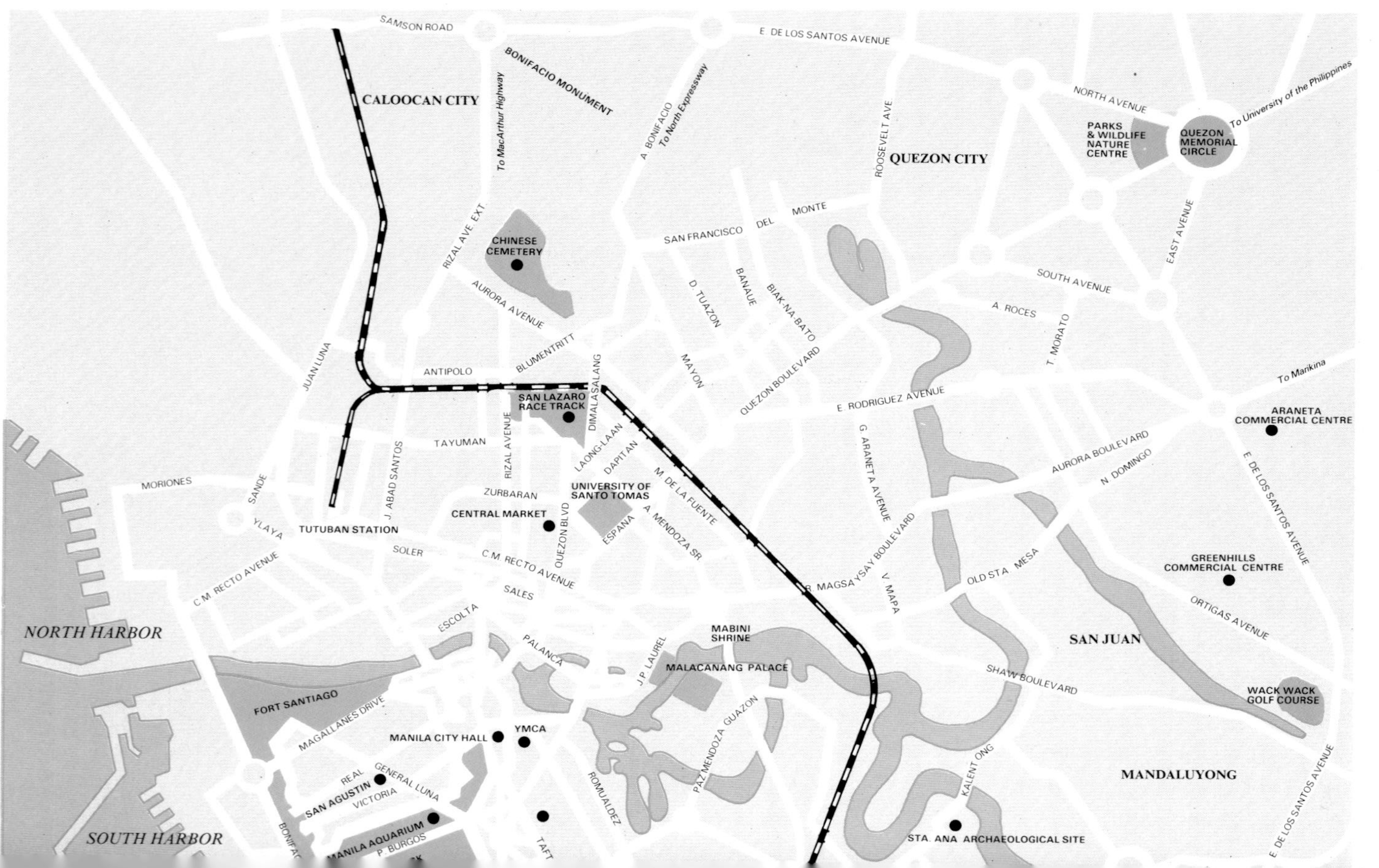

CALOOCAN CITY
SAMSON ROAD
BONIFACIO MONUMENT
To MacArthur Highway
A. BONIFACIO
To North Expressway
E. DE LOS SANTOS AVENUE
ROOSEVELT AVE.
QUEZON CITY
NORTH AVENUE
PARKS & WILDLIFE NATURE CENTRE
QUEZON MEMORIAL CIRCLE
To University of the Philippines
EAST AVENUE
SOUTH AVENUE
A. ROCES
T. MORATO
To Marikina
ARANETA COMMERCIAL CENTRE
RIZAL AVE. EXT.
CHINESE CEMETERY
AURORA AVENUE
SAN FRANCISCO DEL MONTE
D. TUAZON
BANAUE
BIAK-NA-BATO
MAYON
QUEZON BOULEVARD
E. RODRIGUEZ AVENUE
G. ARANETA AVENUE
AURORA BOULEVARD
N. DOMINGO
E. DE LOS SANTOS AVENUE
JUAN LUNA
ANTIPOLO
BLUMENTRITT
DIMALASALANG
SAN LAZARO RACE TRACK
TAYUMAN
RIZAL AVENUE
J. ABAD SANTOS
LAONG-LAAN
DAPITAN
M. DE LA FUENTE
UNIVERSITY OF SANTO TOMAS
MORIONES
SANDE
ZURBARAN
CENTRAL MARKET
QUEZON BLVD
ESPANA
A. MENDOZA SR.
YLAYA
TUTUBAN STATION
SOLER
C.M. RECTO AVENUE
C.M. RECTO AVENUE
SALES
R. MAGSAYSAY BOULEVARD
V. MAPA
OLD STA. MESA
GREENHILLS COMMERCIAL CENTRE
ORTIGAS AVENUE
NORTH HARBOR
ESCOLTA
PALANCA
J.P. LAUREL
MABINI SHRINE
MALACANANG PALACE
SAN JUAN
SHAW BOULEVARD
WACK WACK GOLF COURSE
FORT SANTIAGO
MAGALLANES DRIVE
MANILA CITY HALL
YMCA
PAZ MENDOZA GUAZON
KALENT ONG
REAL
GENERAL LUNA
SAN AGUSTIN
VICTORIA
MANILA AQUARIUM
P. BURGOS
ROMUALDEZ
TAFT
MANDALUYONG
SOUTH HARBOR
STA. ANA ARCHAEOLOGICAL SITE
E. DE LOS SANTOS AVENUE

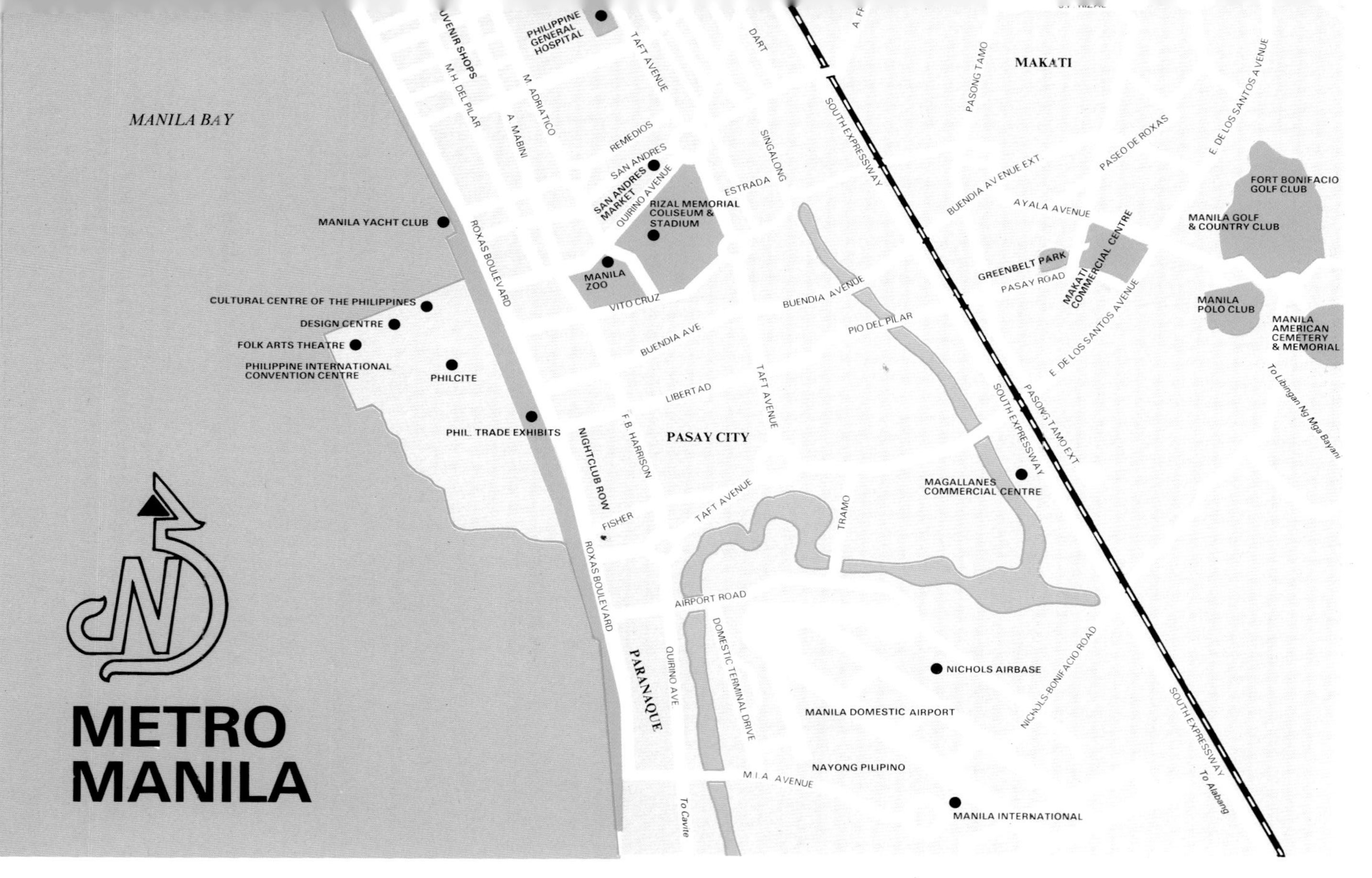

METRO MANILA
MANILA BAY
MAKATI
PASAY CITY
PARANAQUE
MANILA YACHT CLUB
CULTURAL CENTRE OF THE PHILIPPINES
DESIGN CENTRE
FOLK ARTS THEATRE
PHILIPPINE INTERNATIONAL CONVENTION CENTRE
PHILCITE
PHIL. TRADE EXHIBITS
NIGHTCLUB ROW
PHILIPPINE GENERAL HOSPITAL
SAN ANDRES MARKET
RIZAL MEMORIAL COLISEUM & STADIUM
MANILA ZOO
GREENBELT PARK
MAKATI COMMERCIAL CENTRE
FORT BONIFACIO GOLF CLUB
MANILA GOLF & COUNTRY CLUB
MANILA POLO CLUB
MANILA AMERICAN CEMETERY & MEMORIAL
MAGALLANES COMMERCIAL CENTRE
NICHOLS AIRBASE
MANILA DOMESTIC AIRPORT
NAYONG PILIPINO
MANILA INTERNATIONAL
M.H. DEL PILAR
A. MABINI
M. ADRIATICO
TAFT AVENUE
REMEDIOS
SAN ANDRES
QUIRINO AVENUE
ESTRADA
SINGALONG
DART
ROXAS BOULEVARD
VITO CRUZ
BUENDIA AVE
BUENDIA AVENUE
PIO DEL PILAR
LIBERTAD
F.B. HARRISON
FISHER
TRAMO
AIRPORT ROAD
QUIRINO AVE
DOMESTIC TERMINAL DRIVE
M.I.A. AVENUE
To Cavite
SOUTH EXPRESSWAY
PASONG TAMO
PASONG TAMO EXT.
BUENDIA AVENUE EXT
AYALA AVENUE
PASAY ROAD
PASEO DE ROXAS
E. DE LOS SANTOS AVENUE
NICHOLS-BONIFACIO ROAD
To Alabang
To Libingan Ng Mga Bayani

Sulayman commanded his kingdom from a palisaded fort, Spanish conquerors erected a more enduring fortress, **Fort Santiago,** now the premier landmark of historic Manila. Today its partially restored ruins are the setting for a park, a museum and a theatre, but the medieval dungeons used for incarceration and torture throughout its long history remain as grim reminders of the foul deeds of which men are capable. One particularly nasty means of execution was to incarcerate prisoners in dungeons below sea level, their death a certainty as sea gates were opened and high tide rose to ceiling level. National hero Jose Rizal spent the last night of his life here, composing the beautiful *Ultimo Adios* before his execution. Part of the fort is designated the Rizal Shrine.

St Augustine Church, built in 1599 with walls 1.5 metres thick at the base, was the only important structure in Intramuros left standing at the end of World War II. The church's survival through tremendous earthquakes and holocausts is considered the result of divine intervention. It is located at the corner of Gen. Luna Street and Calle Real. (The latter was the city's main street during Spanish times.) Its interior is a marvel of baroque art, featuring a magnificent *trompe-l'oeil* ceiling and fourteen altars. The adjoining monastery contains a museum of religious art and a small library.

The **Manila Metropolitan Cathedral** is also in Intramuros, located between Gen. Luna and Cabildo streets (open daily 8am-8pm). It has been destroyed and rebuilt exactly six times, typhoons, earthquakes, fires and war all taking their toll. Construction of the present cathedral ended in 1958.

Puerta Real, the south gate of Intramuros, leads to the **Manila Aquarium** (open 8am-8pm daily).

Binondo and Quiapo

Across the Pasig River from Intramuros is **Binondo,** Manila's Chinatown. Escolta Street was once the main shopping street of the city and still retains a flavour of old Manila. Ongpin is now the main street of Chinatown, a jungle of Chinese restaurants, jewellery shops, herbalists, movie houses and curio shops. This is the place to rent horse-drawn carriages, which were once the only transportation through the cobblestoned streets. Lovely old **Binondo Church,** fronting Plaza Calderon de la Barca, is worth a visit, as is the **Temple of Ten Thousand Buddhas** on Narra Street.

Not far from Binondo is **Quiapo** district. Its two most famous landmarks are **Quiapo Church,** home of the venerated Black Nazarene, and **Plaza Miranda** fronting the church. Plaza Miranda is traditionally the place where Manilenos bring their grievances and stage their most volatile demonstrations in times of unrest. Probably no political demonstration, though, can equal the fervour of the celebration of the Feast of the Black

Nazarene on January 9 each year, which turns the plaza and surrounding district into a frightening sea of frenzied devotees. The image is venerated every Friday as well, by thousands of worshippers who walk on their knees to the altar.

Outside the church a brisk business in amulets and medicinal herbs flourishes alongside the usual hawkers of flowers and sweepstake tickets. Occupying Quiapo Underpass beneath Plaza Miranda is **Quinta Market,** a great place for poking about and unearthing bargains.

On the south side of Quezon Bridge, at Liwasang Bonifacio, is the **Manila Metropolitan Theatre.** The **Museum of National Costumes** is housed here (open 9am-6pm daily except Mondays). The evolution of Philippine dress is depicted here, including tribal costumes and some dresses from the personal wardrobe of Mrs Marcos, wife of the former president.

Further north from Quiapo, on Espana Street, is the **University of Sto. Tomas.** Dating from 1611, it is the oldest university in the Far East and, as Filipinos love to note, older than Harvard University. The campus sprawls over one city block. Its library has a fine collection of rare books from the 15th through 18th centuries. The university's **Museum of Arts and Sciences** (open 9-11am, 2-4pm, Monday to Friday) is located in the main building.

On the north bank of the Pasig River on Jose P Laurel Street sits **Malacanang Palace.** Dating back to some 200 years, this graceful mansion has housed 14 Spanish governor-generals, 13 American civil governors, and eight Philippines presidents. It was last occupied in February 1986. Its opulent interiors, furnished with crystal chandeliers, priceless paintings and carpets, ornate furniture, and costly porcelains, make it an interesting museum.

Ermita

Extending south from Rizal Park is M.H. del Pilar Street, heart of the Tourist Belt, as the district of Ermita is called. The area is equally intriguing by day or night. A multitude of bars, pubs and restaurants serving every conceivable cuisine makes it a hub of activity after dark. In daylight hours, A. Mabini Street invites leisurely exploration with its rows of shops selling paintings at incredibly low prices, antiques, handicrafts and souvenirs.

Malate Church, built at the end of the 18th century, is one of the oldest churches in Manila. It is located at San Andres Street and M.H. del Pilar Street. Also in the area is the **Carfel Seashell Museum** at 1786 A. Mabini Street (open 8am-7pm Monday to Friday). Some of the world's rarest sea shells are among its extensive collection.

Makati

Makati is the newest commercial hub of Manila, and worth a visit to see its high-rise skyline, drive through its carefully guarded enclaves of luxurious homes and visit the **Makati Commercial Centre,** a giant

shopping complex. The Ayala Museum, one of the best museums in Manila, is located on Makati Avenue (open 9am-6pm daily except Monday). Best among its features are 63 excellent three-dimensional dioramas depicting the unfolding of Philippine history. Its exhibits also include collections of Filipino painters, Filipino costumes, artefacts and rare books. Special cultural presentations are featured on Saturdays. An aviary is situated behind the museum in Greenbelt Park.

The **US Military Cemetery** is inside Fort Bonifacio in Makati. More than 17,000 US military personnel are buried here, all casualties of World War II. A memorial lists the names of more than 36,000 US soldiers missing in action. The park-like landscaping and simple design of its edifices give the cemetery an air of serene beauty.

Other Points of Interest in the City

Santa Ana Church on New Panderos Street is famous for its museum of artefacts discovered in a nearby archaeological site. From behind glass walls, skeletons and pottery remains may be viewed in their original graves.

The **Chinese Cemetery** off Aurora Avenue is a sight not to be missed. Magnificent mausoleums, ranging in design from intricately ornate to strikingly modernistic, have been built by wealthy Chinese families, some equipped with kitchens, bathrooms, electricity and running water. Portraits of the departed and bouquets of plastic flowers are placed at the heads of graves. Thousands of niches in concrete walls serve for the interment of those unable to afford the more luxurious accommodations.

The **Alto Doll Museum** (open 9am-6pm daily) at 400 Guevarra Street has an exhibit of thousands of dolls dressed in authentic costumes of many lands. In addition dolls are shown at work, at play, getting married, doing native dances, participating in cockfights and illustrating all aspects of Philippine life. Dolls are also for sale at the museum.

Located adjacent to Manila International Airport is **Nayong Pilipino** (open 9am-7pm Monday to Thursday, 9am-8pm Friday to Sunday). Nayong Pilipino means Philippine village, and this particular village has the distinction of representing all the major regions of the Philippines, complete with typical architecture, landscape and cultural pursuits, spread over 54 acres of land.

Jeepneys provide transportation between the many regions represented. There is also a Museum of Philippine Traditional Cultures displaying artefacts of the Philippines' minority tribes. Restaurants and shops are found inside the complex.

Manila's Environs

Forty-five minutes from Manila by car, on the main highway of Las Pinas, Rizal, is the **Las Pinas Church** with its famous **Bamboo Organ.** The organ, built in 1822, is the only one of its kind in the world. After years of neglect and the ill effects of time, the organ was finally restored in 1975 and is now featured in an annual Bamboo Organ Festival, with the participation of internationally renowned organists.

Visitors intrigued by the ubiquitous jeepney can watch the vehicles in the making at the **Sarao Jeepney Factory,** where artisans working freehand paint their flamboyant designs on the bodies. The factory is also on the main highway on the way to Las Pinas and the Bamboo Organ (open 8am-noon, 1-5pm daily except Sunday).

Pagsanjan Falls, two hours south of Manila, offers the memorable adventure of going upstream on a river that starts as a placid stream meandering between deep gorges and quickly turns into a churning mass of rapids. Experienced boatmen leap from rock to rock, poling their small *bancas* with their cargo of wide-eyed tourists through the fourteen sets of rapids to reach Pagsanjan Falls.

Once there, you may elect to board a cable-guided raft and go around behind the thundering falls, an experience reminiscent of one of novelist Joseph Conrad's typhoon-at-sea tales. The trip back down the rapids is, needless to say, much faster than the trip up and a good deal more hair-raising. Bathing suits are recommended apparel.

Villa Escudero Plantation and Resort is a self-contained, working coconut plantation 84 kilometres south of Manila near San Pablo City. Attractions include a demonstration of coconut harvesting, a tour of the plantation with a carabao-drawn cart as transportation, lunch at the foot of a waterfall, a swim in a river pool, a ride on a bamboo raft along a jungle stream, guitar-strumming singers, and a private museum reflecting the fascinatingly eclectic taste of the owners. Allow a full day for this one. Especially recommended for children.

Near the town of Alaminos, before reaching San Pablo City, is **Hidden Valley,** a lush resort of natural pools, thermal springs and verdant jungle walks.

From the cool elevation of **Tagaytay Ridge,** 60 kilometres south of Manila, one can enjoy a panoramic view that includes tiny but mighty **Taal Volcano.** Situated on an island in the centre of Taal Lake (which itself is the crater of an extinct volcano), Taal volcano may be reached by motorised *banca* for a closer look unless it is in the throes of one of its frequent tantrums. Taal Vista Lodge is a nearby resort overlooking the lake.

Fifty minutes by hydrofoil from Manila is 'The Rock', the small island of **Corregidor** that guards the entrance to Manila Bay. It was here that Filipino and American forces held off Japanese invading forces for 27 gruelling days before finally capitulating on May 6, 1942. The ghostly ruins of the mile-long barracks still stand, and the famous Malinta Tunnel from which General Douglas MacArthur directed operations may be explored.

The battery on Corregidor

Aside from its historical significance, the small rocky island with its slender beaches, tropical flora and ancient lighthouse is a delight to explore. Hoverferry tours depart from the terminal at the Cultural Centre complex at 8am and 1.30pm. Tours of **Bataan** peninsula (site of the Battle of Bataan) leave from the same terminal. The peninsula has fine beaches near Mariveles.

Shopping

See *What to Buy*, page 44, to get an idea of the Philippines' best products. There are two ways to shop in Manila, in the shopping complexes and tourist centres or in the markets. If you enjoy discovering bargains and entering into negotiations with stall owners eager to make a sale, head for the markets. If you prefer airconditioned comfort and a more relaxed atmosphere, the shopping centres are for you. Small shops where the owner is on the premises offer pleasant and efficient shopping. In larger stores, the lackadaisical service offered and the complexities involved in simply paying for an item (salesgirls seem to be in a permanent state of confusion as to how to write up a sales slip) may drive you to distraction if you're in a hurry.

All shops are open Monday through Saturday; many are open for business on Sunday as well, particularly in the major shopping centres.

Taal Lake and Volcano

Hours are usually from 9.30am to 7.30pm. Small shops sometimes close for lunch, noon-1pm.

Markets

Pistang Pilipino is located between M.H. del Pilar Street and A. Mabini Street in Ermita, near Pedro Gil Street. Nearby is the Flea Market on Roxas Boulevard. Both specialise in Philippine handicraft items. Divisoria Market in San Nicolas is best known for textiles, but carries every conceivable kind of product. Quinta Market under Quezon Bridge in Quiapo is well known for its low prices.

Shopping Centres

A. Mabini and M.H del Pilar and the small streets running between them are good for hours of browsing. Antiques, art works, handicrafts and souvenirs are sold in the hundreds of shops in this area. Escolta in Binondo, formerly Manila's most chic shopping area, still has some first class stores.

Large modern shopping complexes are the Makati Commercial Centre in Makati, Greenhills Shopping Centre in Mandaluyong, Araneta Centre in Quezon City, and Robinson's Commercial Complex behind the Ramada Hotel on A. Adriatico.

Major hotel arcades often have branches of Manila's best-known shops.

Recommended Shops

Antiques
Eleven Ninety One Antiques, 1191 San Marcelino St
Galleon Shop, 1789 M. Adriatico
Likha, 1415 A. Mabini St
Terry's, 1401 A. Mabini St
Art Galleries
ABC Galleries, 2007 A. Mabini St
Hiraya Gallery, 530 UN Ave.
Luz Gallery, 448 Epifanio de los Santos Ave., Makati
Print Collections, 1360 Leon Guinto
Books
Alemar's, 526 UN Ave. and Makati Commercial Centre
Bookmark, 1231 A. Mabini and Makati Commercial Centre
Cigars
Spenders Philippine Cigars, Manila Hilton Hotel (personalised handmade cigars)
Couturiers
(It is advisable to call first for an appointment.)
Ben Ferrales, 1902 M. Adriatico, Tel. 584602
Christian Espiritu, 1776 M. Adriatico, Tel. 593997
Ernest Santiago, 1903 M. Adriatico, Tel. 502926
Pitoy Moreno, 700 Gen. Malvar, Tel. 584794
Romulo Estrada, 1923 San Marcelino, Tel. 506424
Department Stores (Clothing, Filipiana, Cosmetics, Furnishings)
Anson Emporium, Makati and Greenhills Shopping Centres
Rustan's, Makati and Araneta Centre Shopping Centres
Shoemart, Makati and Araneta Centre Shopping Centres
Guitars
Guitarmasters, 385 EDSA
JB Musicmart, Araneta and Robinson's Shopping Centre
Music Centre Philippines, Makati and Araneta Shopping Centres
Handicrafts and Arts
Lawin Cottage Industries, 2-H Sta. Escolastica St
Lina Vizcarra-Oandasan, 2158 G.G. Cruz St (best quality hand embroidery)
T'boli Arts and Crafts, 1362 A. Mabini
Tesoro's, 1325 A. Mabini and Makati Commercial Centre (largest selection of quality handicrafts from all over the Philippines. Ask for a ten percent discount if you pay in cash)
Shells
Carfel Shell Export, 1786 A. Mabini
World of Shells, Makati and Araneta Shopping Centres

Shoes and Bags
Gregg Shoes, 151 N. Domingo St and Makati Commercial Centre
Rustan's Department Store, Makati Commercial Centre
(Also the many shops along Carriedo Street in Quiapo and the entire town of Marikina on the eastern outskirts of Manila.)

Restaurants

Manila is home to hundreds of restaurants specialising in every conceivable type of cuisine, as is fitting in a city where food is a major preoccupation of the residents. The listing that follows is a mere sampling of some of the finest in their categories. If you're still undecided, cruise up and down Pasay Road and Makati Avenue in Makati or walk around Ermita, districts where restaurants line the streets, one after another.

Seafood and Filipino

As seafood is a staple of the Filipino diet, it is often a speciality of restaurants offering native cooking.

Bahia Seafood Restaurant—Hotel Inter-Continental Manila, Ayala Avenue, Makati (Tel. 8159711). International menu, musical entertainment.

Bangus—1006 Pasay Road, Makati (Tel. 854645). Very small, serves *bangus*, the native milkfish, in dozens of different ways.

The Grove—5003 P. Burgos Street, Makati (Tel. 898383). Extensive variety of regional native dishes. Option of choosing food *turo-turo* (literally, 'point-point') style from a cafeteria-like selection.

Josephine's—1800 Roxas Blvd, Pasay (Tel. 591550). Branch at Greenbelt Park, Makati (Tel. 868835). Old-established and popular seafood restaurant chain.

Maynila—The Manila Hotel, Rizal Park (Tel. 573711). Turn-of-the-century elegance. Filipino menu. Performances of native song and dance.

Pier 7—Philippine Plaza Hotel, Roxas Boulevard, Manila (Tel. 8320701). Seafood and steaks; international buffet lunch.

Sinugba—800 Pasay Road, Makati (Tel. 880298). Seafood and Cebuano specialities eaten in the *kamayan* style.

Sulu Restaurant—Makati Commercial Centre (Tel. 8185011). Native dishes and an exuberant floor show of native folk dances.

Tito Rey—Amorsolo Street, corner Pasay Road, Makati (Tel. 854781). One of the best of the *kamayan* (eat with your fingers) restaurants.

Via Mare—Greenbelt Square, Makati (Tel. 852306). Tops in its category. Has a separate oyster bar. Expensive.

Zamboanga—8739 Makati Avenue, Makati (Tel. 894932). Speciality is deep-sea crabs caught in waters off Zamboanga.

The Hundred Islands

Chinese

In Binondo, Manila's Chinatown, two restaurants with little atmosphere, but excellent Chinese food, are: **New Carvajal** at 636 Carvajal Street (Tel. 4882770), and **See Kee** at 833 Ongpin Street (Tel. 481934).

Primarily Cantonese food, plusher atmosphere, is found at the following restaurants:

Lotus Garden—Manila Midtown, Pedro Gil corner M. Adriatico, Ermita (Tel. 573911).

The Peacock—Century Park Sheraton, Vito Cruz, Manila (Tel. 506041).

Japanese

Aoi—Century Park Sheraton, Vito Cruz, Manila (Tel. 506041).

Kaneko—Makati Avenue, Makati (Tel. 854414).

Gojinka—Manila Garden Hotel, Makati Commercial Centre, Makati (Tel. 857911).

Kiku—Manila Midtown Hotel, Pedro Gil corner M. Adriatico, Ermita (Tel. 573911).

New Tokyo House—691 Makati Avenue, Makati (Tel. 871153).

Indian

Kashmir Indian Cuisine—Mabini, corner Padre Faura, Ermita (Tel. 506851).

India House Restaurant—1718 M. Adriatico Street, Malate (Tel. 572560).

Spanish

Alba Patio de Makati—8751 Paseo de Roxas, Makati, 11th floor (Tel. 862341). Moorish decor, excellent Castilian cuisine.

Casa Marcos—Roxas Blvd. Ext., Paranaque (Tel. 8310915). Steaks a speciality, as well as Spanish cuisine.

Guernica's—1326 M.H. del Pilar, Ermita (Tel. 500936). Spanish taverna atmosphere.

La Tasca—Greenbelt Park, Makati (Tel. 868541).

Madrid—24-25 EDSA, Mandaluyong (Tel. 797561). Elegant, formal European atmosphere. Music in the evening.

Mario's—7856 Makati Avenue, Makati (Tel. 864478). Intimate atmosphere.

Patio Guernica—1856 Jorge Bocobo Street, Ermita (Tel. 5214415).

French and Continental

Au Bon Vivant—1133 L. Guerrero Street, Ermita (Tel. 503840). Long-time favourite for French cuisine in Manila.

Champagne Room—Manila Hotel, Rizal Park (Tel. 573711). Formal dining. String musicians.

Hugo's—Hyatt Regency Manila, Roxas Blvd (Tel. 8312611). Excellent food in a luxurious atmosphere. German specialities. Strolling quartet.

La Table Du Baron—Holiday Inn, Roxas Blvd (Tel. 595961). Gourmet French cuisine in a Louis XIII atmosphere.

L'Orangerie—89 Zodiac Street, Bel-Air IV, Makati (Tel. 878939). Nouvelle cuisine.

Prince Albert Rotisserie—Hotel Inter-Continental, Makati Commercial Centre (Tel. 8159711). Plush atmosphere, fine wines, continental menu.

Top of the Hilton—Manila Hilton, UN Avenue (Tel. 573711). Great view of Manila. Continental menu.

Italian

Di' Mark's—7841 Makati Avenue, Makati (Tel. 8188868).

Italian Village—7853 Makati Avenue, Makati (Tel. 876623).

La Taverna—1602 M. Adriatico Street, Ermita (Tel. 585372).

Pizza Hut—McKinley Road, Greenhills (Tel. 9216891).

Other

Al Berdoni—1619 M. Adriatico, Ermita (above Zamboanga restaurant). Lebanese food and entertainment.

Alfredo's Steak House—Tomas Morato Avenue, Quezon City (Tel. 976026).

Luau—7829 Makati Avenue, Makati (Tel. 879543).

Nina's Papagayo—Makati Avenue, corner Anza Street, Makati (Tel. 8161935). Mexican food, guitarists.

Tia Maria Mexican Restaurant—7829 Makati Avenue, Makati (Tel. 875931).

Cafes, Pubs and Nightspots

M.H. del Pilar, A. Mabini and nearby streets in Ermita's 'tourist belt' come alive at night with dozens of pubs, clubs and bars. A stroll around the area will give you an idea of the variety of entertainment available—anything from intimate European-style cafes to bawdy 'hospitality girl' establishments. For bigger cabarets and nightspots, sample the neon row along Roxas Boulevard. Makati also has its fair share of establishments offering quiet or raucous evenings, as you prefer. A few of the well-known nightspots are mentioned here:

Bayside—Roxas Blvd. (This one's been around for donkey's years and is still going strong. 'Hostesses' available for the lone male.)

Bistro Burgos—P. Burgos, Makati. (Cosy, intimate.)

Cafe Adriatico—M. Adriatico, Malate. (Light classical taped background music.)

Eduardo's—Roxas Blvd. (Supper club featuring top Filipino artists.)

Firehouse—M.H. del Pilar Ermita. (Go-go dancers.)

Guernica's—M.H. del Pilar Street. (Of long-standing popularity. Sing along with the convivial crowd in a Spanish ambience.)

The Hobbit House—A. Mabini, Ermita. (Staffed by dwarfs. Good live folk and pop music.)

Kangaroo Club—United Nations Avenue, Ermita. (Australian-style pub.)

Moviola—M. Adriatico, Malate. (Intimate cafe. 'Hollywood greats' decor. Pianist.)

My Father's Moustache—M.H. del Pilar, Ermita. (Folk singing.)

Orchid Bar—Manila Midtown Hotel, Pedro Gil and M. Adriatico. (Lobby bar, open 24 hours. Soft piano music.)

Rodeo Drive—Makati Avenue, Makati. (Cowboy music, mechanical bull.)

San Mig Pub—Geenbelt Park, Makati. (A pub, as one might guess, named for the Philippines' justifiably famous San Miguel beer.)

Discos

Altitude 49—Manila Garden Hotel, Makati Commercial Centre, Makati.

Apres—Manila Hotel, Rizal Park.
La Cueva—Greenbelt Park, Makati.
Lost Horizon—Philippine Plaza Hotel, Cultural Centre Complex, Roxas Blvd.
Penthouse Disco—Ambassador Hotel, A. Mabini Street, Malate.
Queue—Regent of Manila, Roxas Blvd.
Stargazer Lounge—19th Floor, Silahis International Hotel, Roxas Blvd.

Manila Bay Casino

In a class by itself is the Manila Bay Casino, located at the mezzanine of the Philippine Village Hotel. It is open at all hours seven days a week, and entrance is free to all tourists upon presentation of passports. Dining and drinking can be combined with the excitement of the gaming tables.

Metro Manila Hotels

The following four hotels are located in Makati, the business centre of Metro Manila, and are within a few blocks of each other and of the huge Makati Commercial Shopping Centre:
Manila Peninsula—Corner Makati Avenue & Ayala Avenue (Tel. 8193456).
Manila Mandarin—Corner Makati Avenue & Paseo de Roxas (Tel. 8163601).
Manila Garden Hotel—EDSA Highway (Tel. 857911).
Hotel Inter-Continental Makati Commercial Centre (Tel. 8159711).
The following hotels are in or near the heart of the tourist district along Roxas Boulevard and in Ermita.
Century Park Sheraton—Vito Cruz (Tel. 506041).
Holiday Inn Manila—Roxas Blvd (Tel. 597961).
Silahis International Hotel—Roxas Blvd (Tel. 573811).
The Regent of Manila—Roxas Blvd (Tel. 8310001).
Hyatt Regency Manila—Roxas Blvd (Tel. 8312611).
Manila Hilton International—United Nations Avenue (Tel. 573711).
The Philippine Plaza—Roxas Blvd (Tel. 8320701). Situated on reclaimed land extending out into Manila Bay. It could easily classify as a resort in itself: spacious, beautifully landscaped grounds, tennis courts, putting green, and a spectacular pool.
Manila Midtown Hotel—Corner Pedro Gil and M. Adriatico (Tel. 573911). This hotel recently separated from its affiliation with Ramada Inns and has undergone extensive renovations. Situated in a large complex of shops and commercial facilities.
The Manila Hotel—Rizal Park (Tel. 470011). One of Asia's finest hotels, rich in history, overlooking Manila Bay.

The Philippine Village Hotel—Nayong Pilipino (Tel. 8317011). Government-operated, near Manila International Airport and the Nayong Pilipino cultural park.

Southern Luzon

The Bicol peninsula is attached like an afterthought to the east coast of southern Luzon. Like the rest of the Philippines, the entire region is rich in scenic beauty, but the star attraction is undoubtedly **Mayon Volcano,** whose name is taken from the local word for 'beautiful'. Majestic is another word aptly describing this towering giant whose slopes rise in gentle symmetry from the surrounding plain to a perfect cone.

Legazpi

The usual base for exploring Bicol is Legazpi City, provincial capital of Albay. Just a few kilometres outside the city are the ruins of **Kagsawa Church,** mute testament to Mayon's destructive force. Of the more than forty recorded eruptions, one of the worst occurred in 1814 when the town of Kagsawa was buried under tons of rock, lava and earth. Only the blackened belfry of the church remains to be seen, thrusting up from a sea of lava rock. Wisps of smoke and steam rising intermittently from Mayon in the background are sobering reminders that the volcano is only resting.

Guided treks take the adventurous and energetic traveller right to the summit of Mayon during the dry season. (See *Sports,* page 72). A commanding view of the surrounding countryside and a disquieting feeling of being directly under the towering cone can be had from the **Mayon Resthouse,** about a third of the way up the volcano at 800 metres above sea level and accessible by road.

About fifteen kilometres from Legazpi are the **Hoyop-Hoyopan Caves,** part of an extensive series of limestone caves in the region. Guides take visitors through the labyrinth of weirdly-shaped stalagmites and multiple entrances. The caves were used by Filipino guerillas during World War II to elude the Japanese. They have since served a happier purpose when young people evaded the curfew law during the years of martial law by turning one of the main chambers into a discotheque.

Tiwi Hot Springs are 44 kilometres north of Legazpi. The whole area is a sulphurous, bubbling cauldron of geothermal activity. Visitors can bathe in the warm waters, pick their way along the edges of boiling hot springs at Naglabong, and visit the Tiwi Geothermal Power Plant.

Just west of Tiwi, in the province of Camarines Sur, is **Lake Buhi,** where the world's smallest fish are netted. So tiny as to be transparent, the dot-sized *tabios* are served up in a 'thousand-fish omelette' at the nearby Ibalon Hotel. Camarines Sur is noted for its old Spanish churches, of which the **cathedral at Naga,** the provincial capital, is an outstanding example.

South from Albay is Sorsogon province, site of **Bulusan Volcano** and its lovely crater lake surrounded by a forest lush with orchids, ferns and jungle vegetation. Catanduanes island, east of the Bicol peninsula, and Masbate island, at its southwestern end, boast some of the finest beaches in the Philippines.

The five-star Mayon Imperial Hotel, situated on a hillside overlooking Legazpi, has excellent facilities. A few kilometres outside the city is Kagayonan Resort Hotel, offering two swimming pools and a black sand beach. Inside the city is centrally located Hotel La Trinidad, which has a swimming pool and good restaurants.

Northern Luzon

Baguio

Dubbed the summer capital of the Philippines, Baguio nestles 5,000 feet above sea level in the pine-covered hills of Luzon's Cordillera

Baguio Cathedral

mountain range. It was little more than an Igorot settlement until the turn of the century when the Americans, in the tradition of colonialists all over Asia, decided to build a resort to escape the sultry summers of the lowlands. What they built was a replica of an Adirondacks village—big summer houses with clapboard siding, shuttered windows and wrap-around porches; gardens ablaze with flowers common to temperate climates; small parks and statuary scattered throughout the city, and a prevailing air of neatness and order.

In spite of new hotels and high-rise buildings, Baguio's leisurely charm has been retained. It is still the number one vacation destination of both Filipinos and resident foreigners. During the Easter holiday, its population of 100,000 is tripled as vacationers pour into the city to enjoy forest strolls, horseback riding, golf and the pleasure (rare in the tropics) of curling up in front of pine-scented fires in the cool evenings.

Churches of every denomination, convents and seminaries dot the hills, reflecting the city's ecumenical spirit. Faith healers abound as well, of whom Tony Agpaoa was the most famous until his death in 1982. He purchased a complex of buildings on Dominican Hill, one of Baguio's landmarks, and transformed it into a hotel cum hospital known as the Diplomat Hotel. Agpaoa received visitors from all over the world who arrived, often by chartered planeloads, in last-ditch attempts to find restored health. Faith healer Jun Labo is the current favourite in the city, following in Agpaoa's footsteps by operating his own hotel healing centre, the Nagoya Inn.

Baguio is not only a religious centre, but an educational centre boasting six colleges and universities. Among them is the Philippine Military Academy, where parades by smartly uniformed cadets may be witnessed on weekends.

Things to See and Do

There are a number of interesting things to do and see in the city if you can overcome the inclination to simply relax and laze about in the morning hour.

Before you start your tour, it's advisable to stop by the Ministry of Tourism office located in the Baguio Tourism Complex on Governor Pack Road and pick up a map of the city. The maze of roads that meander through the hills can be disorienting, especially for nighttime drivers who, unless skilled in celestial navigation, may end up going in circles.

Inside the **Baguio Tourism Complex** is a very nice little museum with displays of artefacts which are a good introduction to the customs and traditions of the various tribes of Mountain province. Behind the museum is **Baguio Sunshine Park,** a garden of flowers where cultural shows are often presented.

A short distance away, on Leonard Wood Road, **Imelda Park** features prototypes of dwellings of the various mountain tribes in a natural woodland setting. Costumed tribespeople greet visitors at the entrance.

Session Road is the main street of the city. Strolling up and down its steep length is the major occupation of many visitors. The street is a hotchpotch of little shops, restaurants, banks and movie houses. Just up a flight of steps from Session Road is the **Baguio Cathedral,** whose twin spires and tolling of the angelus every evening at 6pm have become familiar symbols of the city.

At the foot of Session Road is the **public market,** billed as one of the cleanest in Asia, and not to be missed. Here the occasional G-stringed man or tattooed, cigar-smoking woman, old folks from the mountain tribes, may be seen selling their produce. The vegetables, of a crisp freshness seldom seen in Manila, come from nearby La Trinidad, the fertile valley known as the salad bowl of the Philippines. In the fruit section, displays of mangoes, lanzones, apples and papaya all pale into the ordinary when placed alongside Baguio's most famous fruit, strawberries. Careful arrangements of woven baskets piled high with the red, luscious berries make still-life pictures of mouth-watering beauty. Above the fruit and vegetable displays, jars of strawberry and blueberry jam share shelf space with peanut brittle, another Baguio speciality.

But the fruits, vegetables and viands are only a small part of what the market has to offer. Woodcarvings, baskets, handwoven fabrics, antiques (fake and genuine), silver filigree jewellery, tawdry 'souvenirs' of every variety, flowers—from fresh red roses to the dried 'everlasting' variety—stacks of fan-shaped grass brooms, army surplus goods, beads and blankets all serve to keep shoppers fascinated for hours. Small 'carry-your-bag' boys will do just that for a few coins.

Along Abad Santos Drive is **Burnham Park,** named after Daniel Burnham, the American architect who designed the city. Here you may rent boats to row across the shallow waters of placid man-made lake surrounded by weeping willows. A playground for children is nearby.

The Mansion is the name given to the summer residence of the president. Originally built to house the American governors-generals, its most interesting feature is its main gate, a replica of the one at Buckingham Palace. Across the road from The Mansion is a flower-boardered reflecting pool which leads to a promontory overlooking Wright Park and its herd of riding horses. The horses, sturdy little beasts in spite of their diminutive size, may be rented by the hour.

John Hay Air Base, at the southeastern edge of the city, was built as a recreational camp for US military families, but is now largely open to the public. It has bowling alleys, tennis courts, well-marked hiking trails, a children's playground and a skating rink. The number one sports attraction, though, is its challenging golf course. Hole number three is

dubbed 'Cardiac Hill', which gives some idea of the terrain. John Hay's beautifully manicured grounds and pretty little white cottages make it a pleasure to visit, if only to stop by for an American-style hamburger at the 19th Tee restaurant.

There are several scenic spots around the city that offer superb panoramas of the surrounding mountains. One is the above-mentioned **Dominican Hill.** On a knoll opposite Dominican Hill is **Mirador Hill,** site of a Jesuit-owned retreat centre. In addition to its unobstructed view all the way to the China Sea, Mirador Hill is the site of **Lourdes Grotto,** a religious shrine that is packed with devotees during Holy Week. A flight of steps, 225 of them, leads to an image of Our Lady of Lourdes. Another well-known lookout point is **Mines View Park,** whose former atmosphere of peaceful isolation has been lost in a tangle of souvenir stalls. In addition, it is so small and generally crowded that one fears being elbowed over the cliff into the mines below.

At the boundary of Baguio City and La Trinidad is **Bell Church,** a cluster of temples where the priests practise their unusual blend of Taoism, Confucianism, Buddhism and Christianity. Do-it-yourself fortune telling is possible here by following the prescribed procedure posted at the altars. Light some incense, shake bamboo divination sticks out of a round container, and look up the interpretation of signs in a book placed handily nearby for the purpose.

A few kilometres beyond Bell Church, the road angles sharply to the right just in front of the **Benguet Provincial Capitol.** There is a small, interesting museum on the capitol grounds, but upstairs in the provincial governor's office are perhaps the most unusual museum pieces. They are three mummies in glass cases, relics of the tribal burial practice of seating the dead on chairs and smoking them until the remains were mummified.

One of the pleasures Baguio offers is the opportunity to observe handicrafts in the making. Colourful, geometric Igorot patterns are produced on handlooms at the **Easter School of Weaving** on Bokawkan Road. At **Narda's Knitting and Weaving** in La Trinidad (about 15 minutes from Baguio), beautiful contemporary *ikat* weave wall hangings, rugs, place-mats and handbags are made. The entire process—tie-dyeing the yarns, weaving and finishing—may be observed on the premises. On the building's rooftop are two authentic Igorot dwellings, brought down intact from remote mountain areas. One was the birthplace of the shop's owner. Finished woven products are for sale at both Narda's and the Easter School.

The **St Louis University Trade School** produces delicate silver filigree jewellery and art objects. Finest quality workmanship and honest pricing are guaranteed at this trade school run by nuns. Visitors to the workshop are welcome.

Off Naguilian Road, leading west out of Baguio towards the town of Asin, is the site of **'woodcarvers village',** clusters of dwellings where whole families, including small children, work at their ancestral skill of producing woodcarvings. Prices here are generally lower than in town, but bargaining is required. Continuing on the same road will bring you to Peter L. Pinder's Leathercraft, where fine quality hand-tooled leather products are made and sold by a young Englishman and his wife. And travelling even further along this road, a total of 15 kilometres from Baguio, will bring you to **Asin Hot Springs Resort,** where there are changing rooms and swimming pools fed by the hot springs.

Shopping

Session Road, City Market and its adjoining two-storey concrete shopping complex, Maharlika, are good territories to explore for antiques, silver filigree work, jars, baskets and other ethnic handicrafts. The textiles from Narda's and the Easter Weaving School are available in shops in the Hyatt Terraces Baguio Hotel and the Resort Pines Hotel, as well as at their workshop sites.

A shop adjoining the Munsayoc's Holiday Inn on Leonard Wood Road has a large and excellent stock of woodcarvings and basketry.

Baskets and woven bamboo items of every description are the speciality of Baguio Bamboo Handicrafts at 10 Laubach Road.

Ceferina's Bamboo & Rattan Crafts Shop on Leonard Wood Road carries an extensive collection of native-style baskets and carvings plus a few pieces of antique furniture, some genuine and some eye-deceiving copies. The owner is scrupulous about pointing out which is which.

Hotels and Restaurants

Hyatt Terraces Baguio (Tel. 4425670; 4425780) is a five-star hotel, the finest in the city. It has a very good Japanese restaurant, the Hanazono, international food in the Copper Grill, the Gold Mine discotheque, and L'Atelier Cellar Bar.

The **Resort Pines Hotel** (Tel. 44250200) is a venerable Baguio institution. Among its attractions are a discotheque, the Sandiwa, and a casino.

The new **Baguio Park Hotel** (Tel. 4425626) is more centrally located, on Harrison Road just across from Burnham Park.

Casa Mario is an excellent Spanish restaurant on Session Road. Chinese restaurants, also on Session Road, are the **Star Cafe** and the **Session Cafe. Fernande's** on Carino Street offers French cuisine and Mexican food is the speciality of the **Lone Star Restaurant** at John Hay Air Base.

Folk music is the main fare offered at the **Country Tavern Folkhouse,** the **Fire Place** and the **Gingerbread Man.** The latter can be a bit raucous.

Banaue

A long trip over mountain roads ends in one of the most spectacular and renowned sights in the Philippines, the **Banaue Rice Terraces.** The work of Ifugaos more than 2,000 years ago, the terraces rise in a mosaic of greens and browns, encircling entire mountains, and undulate away to the horizon in silent, awesome beauty. The magnitude of the feat can be appreciated when one realises that only the most primitive tools were used to carve this 10,400 square kilometres of cultivale land out of hostile terrain.

Interesting aspects of Ifugao culture may be seen in nearby villages, some of which are reached by exhilarating hikes of varying duration over mountain trails.

There is an **Ifugao market** near the hotel and a new **Banaue Trade Centre** just across from the market.

The two best places to stay require advance reservations, particularly during the peak months from December to April. The **Banaue Hotel** is a well-equipped hotel with a restaurant, swimming pool and nightly cultural presentations in the lobby. The alternative is the **Banaue Youth Hostel,** which offers dormitory-style accommodation (one wing for women, the other for men) and meals served in the dining room on a specific schedule.

Banaue can be reached from Manila or Baguio, both routes taking between eight and nine hours. The approach from Baguio over the rugged Halsema Mountain Highway makes a rougher, but more interesting trip. This route, snaking around mountains high above verdant valleys and cascading waterfalls, reaches 2,220 metres at its highest point. The **Ambuklao Dam** and reservoir may be seen from the highway. A short side trip can be made to the small town of Sagada, where the chief attractions are the hanging coffins in the burial caves of the nearby limestone hills. The town of **Kabayan,** also reached by a road forking off Halsema Highway, is the site of more **burial caves.** The mummies, their tattoo marks still visible after 500 years, lie crouched inside tree trunk coffins.

La Union

La Union and Ilocos Sur are provinces on the northwestern coast of Luzon. The capital of La Union is San Fernando, but tourists usually head for the nearby town of Bauang, where hotels and resorts proliferate along stretches of sandy beaches. Local boatmen charge a standard fee to carry scuba divers to the choicest spots for diving. Resort hotels have their own restaurants, swimming pools and water sports equipment for rental.

San Fernando's market has a variety of handicrafts, the best buy being

the lightweight Ilocano blankets which are the speciality of the region.

Fresh seafood is the obvious choice for good dining here. A local speciality called *kilawin* is similar to the Mexican *seviche*, raw fish pickled in a spicy vinegar marinade.

Better class resort hotels in Bauang are the **Nalinac** (Tel. 2402; 2460), **Cresta Ola** (Tel. 2983) and **Sun Valley** (Tel. 2745).

La Union is ninety minutes by car or bus from Baguio, and a frequent destination of day trippers who come down to enjoy the sand and sun and then hurry back to Baguio's cool recesses. Jeepneys also make the trip every 30 minutes from the corner of Abanao and Chugum streets in Baguio. From Manila, travel time by bus (Pantranco or Philippine Rabbit) or car is between four and five hours, depending on traffic. Getting from one town to the next is a simple matter, as the towns are clustered in a row along the main highway. Just step out and hail a jeepney. **Agoo,** which has an imposing basilica fronting the town plaza and a pretty park, Imelda Garden, is 20 minutes from Bauang, while San Fernando, the provincial capital, is a mere five minutes distant.

Vigan

A long drive up the coast, almost four hours beyond La Union, is Vigan, the capital of Ilocos Sur. Going to Vigan is stepping into the Spanish colonial past. Gracious old brick and wood houses with hanging balconies, multi-paned capiz shell windows and high-arched carriage entrances line the streets of the '*mestizo* quarter', built when wealthy Chinese *mestizos* composed the aristocracy of the city. Horse-drawn *calesas* and the occasional bullock cart clip-clop over cobblestone streets, unperturbed by the motorcycles and pedicabs, intruders from the present, that zoom past with an unseemly roar.

The city was founded by Juan de Salcedo, grandson of Legazpi, who attempted to duplicate the Intramuros (walled city) section of Manila. A walking tour of Vigan thus gives a glimpse into the vanished past of Manila as well. A monument to De Salcedo adorns the city plaza.

Vigan was the home town of Father Jose Burgos, martyred priest of Spanish times. His former residence now houses the **Ayala Museum,** containing a collection of Ilocano native artefacts and antiques serving to remind that other cultures, rich and colourful, predated the Spaniards in this region.

Syguia Mansion on Quirino Avenue, a fine example of 19th century colonial architecture, is open to the public. It now houses memorabilia of former President Elpidio Quirino, a one-time resident.

One of the loveliest landmarks in Vigan is **St Paul's Cathedral,** facing Salcedo Plaza, the centre of the city. It was originally built in 1574, then went through a ten-year rebuilding period that ended in 1800. Its graceful cream and white facade is an exception to the usual weathered stone exteriors of old Spanish churches in the Philippines. A dazzling feature of the cathedral's interior is its huge main altar, faced in panels of intricately designed beaten silver.

Also on Salcedo Plaza is St Joseph's Antique Shop, which enjoys a reputation for quality merchandise and reliability. Browsers are welcome.

The predominant feature of the Ilocos landscape is its many old churches, their massive buttressed architectural style dubbed 'earthquake baroque'. Almost every town square has its sturdy edifice, designed to withstand earthquakes and the ravages of time. These churches, built with forced labour, were intended to bring the native population *bajo de las campanas* (under the bells). Just south of Vigan, overlooking a vast plaza in the town of Bantay, is **Bantay Church.** This is a notable departure from the general baroque of the region in that it incorporates Gothic touches as well.

North from Vigan on the way to Laoag, capital of Ilocos Norte, interesting churches worth a visit are found in the towns of **Magsingal, San Juan, Cabugao** and **Badoc.** The town of **Paoay,** 20 kilometres south of Laoag, claims the most famous church in the region. Its curious blend of the baroque and the oriental has resulted in a stunning and unique architectural achievement.

Laoag Cathedral is another beautiful old structure with capiz shell windows. The bell tower, which has sunk due to frequent earthquake activity, is set several metres away from the church.

East from Laoag is **Sarrat,** birthplace of former President, Mr Ferdinand E Marcos. The house where he was born is now preserved as the **Marcos Museum,** and contains memorabilia of the presient and his family. The old family manse has undergone considerable alterations in recent years, historical accuracy apparently being less importance than impressive appearance. Nearby **Sarrat Church and Convent** are good examples of colonial period architecture.

Vigan Hotel (Tel. 661), a 300-year-old former private mansion, and the **Cordillera Inn** (Tel. 233) offer good accommodation in the city.

The Visayas

Cebu

The key word for Cebu City, capital of Cebu island and second largest city in the Philippines, is 'oldest'. It not only describes the city, but many of its famous landmarks and antiquities. An Old World air pervades the city in spite of its size. Part of its charm is visual—the small parks, old fort and tree-lined streets spread at the foot of undulating hills. The residents

MAGELLAN'S CROSS
THIS CROSS OF TINDALO WOOD
ENCASES THE ORIGINAL CROSS PLANTED
BY FERDINAND MAGELLAN ON THIS VERY SITE
APRIL 21, 1521
THIS MARKER IS DONATED BY
THE CEBU TOURIST

provide the balance of the charm with their unhurried graciousness and ready smiles.

It was here that Magellan came ashore and performed his famous baptism of 800, including Rajah Humabon and Queen Juana, introducing Christianity to the Philippines. The site of this historic event is marked by a kiosk-like structure at city centre, said to contain the original **cross planted by Magellan.** In 1834 the cross was encased in another hollow wooden cross to prevent its eventual disappearance due to devotees' habit of carrying off bits and pieces as talismans. Present-day visitors are confined to lighting candles, sold at the entrance to the small kiosk, and kneeling in prayer at the foot of the cross.

Nearby is the **Basilica Minore del Santo Nino,** formerly known as San Agustin Church. It was built in 1565 to house the country's most celebrated religious relic, a small statue of the Santo Nino, patron saint of Cebu, said to have been Magellan's baptismal gift to Queen Juana. The statue is encased in a glass shrine bathed in eerie green light off to the left of the main altar. A constant line of devotees files through to kiss the relic at the foot of the statue and offer prayers. Outside the church, the worshipper pressed for time may hire one of the old women there who offer a unique service. For a small fee, she will pray fervently on your behalf while moving in a slow, rhythmic dance step and holding a lighted candle before her.

The first two weeks of January are dedicated to the Santo Nino, a time when the streets of the city become impassable as pilgrims pour in from all over the country, many content to sleep on mats along the sidewalks around the basilica for lack of better accommodation.

Not far from the basilica is **Fort San Pedro,** oldest in the Philippines. The triangular fort has a varied history, beginning in 1565 when it was a mere wooden stockade built for Legazpi's soldiers. This was soon replaced by the present structure, built of coral stone with walls 20 feet high and 18 feet thick, topped by three watch-towers where Spanish soldiers maintained 24-hour guard against possible insurrection. At the time of construction the fort sat directly on the waterfront, but its rusting cannons and nearby statue of a solemn Pigafetta, Magellan's chronicler, now look out over the wharves of the port. Legazpi's statue stands guard in the grounds on the opposite side of the fort. After suffering through occupation by Americans, Japanese, government warehouses and a short-lived zoo, the fort was declared a national shrine and now encloses tranquil gardens.

A short walk from the fort is **Plaza Independencia,** a pleasant little park dominated by an obelisk honouring Legazpi. A bit further on is Colon Street, oldest in the country, although no sign of its antiquity remains in the uninteresting facades of shops, banks and department stores lining its narrow width. The tangle of vehicles along this street, the heart of the city, makes Manila's traffic look the picture of civilised order by comparison.

Colon Street was formerly known as the Parian, the name given to

Cebu's Chinatown district, where Chinese residents were contained in accordance with the Spaniards' practice of ethnic segregation. (It was Spanish colonial practice for the Europeans to occupy the major and best part of the cities, while the Chinese were restricted to a separate section and the rest was left to the 'Indios', the Filipinos.) A newly restored 19th century Parian residence, its interior furnished in authentic antiques, was opened to the public at the beginning of 1984. A walk through the house, **Casa Gorordo,** is to glimpse the elegant and leisurely lifestyle of Cebu's wealthy upper class of the period.

The Avenue of Nations, a pretty tree-lined street, starts at Fuente Osmena, a central rotunda, and leads to Cebu's gleaming domed provincial **capitol building,** perhaps one of the most imposing in the nation. The Palace of Justice lies just behind the capitol.

High on a hill near the exclusive subdivision of Beverly Hills is a **Taoist Temple,** an architectural landmark where the teachings of the Chinese philosopher Lao-tse are preserved. The panoramic view of the city below, Mactan island and the strait between is one of the best in Cebu.

Cebu is the educational centre of the south, with more than twenty colleges and universities. Its **San Carlos University,** said to be the oldest in the Philippines, houses a small **museum** which is open to the public.

Art fanciers may appreciate a visit to the home and gallery of **Julian Jumalon** at 754 Tres de Abril Street. Jumalon, a professor of biology and an artist, creates arresting pictures and portraits using butterfly wings as his medium. His work is sought after, expensive and increasingly rare. A well-travelled and articulate old gentleman, Jumalon may be induced to tell the interesting story of how he came to be the master of his unique form of art, and will perhaps show you around his garden where he cultivates not flowers, but butterflies.

The airport serving Cebu is located on Mactan island, connected by a modern bridge. En route to Cebu from Mactan, one passes through Mandaue City where 300-year-old St Joseph Church houses a life-size tableau of the Last Supper. During Lent this parish stages a 24-hour passion play depicting the last days of Christ.

Along the highway near the Mactan end of the bridge are the factories where the island's most famous export, handmade guitars of excellent quality, are produced. Visitors are welcome at the workshops.

Lapu Lapu City is Mactan's capital, named after the chieftain who brought about Magellan's untimely demise. Both antagonists are honoured at the alleged seaside site of the deed, Magellan with a marker monument and Lapu Lapu with a statue of astonishing proportions. Nearby stalls offer for sale a rich assortment of shells from the surrounding seas.

Beach and diving resorts on Cebu and Mactan are among the Philippines' best, and a major tourist attraction. For a listing of the most popular, see the *Resorts* section, page 76.

Hotels

The **Cebu Plaza** (Tel. 61630) on the outskirts of the city is a five-star hotel that has a swimming pool, tennis courts, an attached casino and a great view.

The **Montebello Villa** (Tel. 85021) was a former private club and is now a four-star hotel. Its Spanish-style architecture, sprawling grounds (including two swimming pools) and family atmosphere give it a distinct charm.

The **Magellan International** (Tel. 74611) on Gorordo Avenue is a centrally located four-star hotel that offers guests playing rights on an 18-hole golf course at the rear.

Restaurants and Nightlife

For traditional Filipino food eaten *kamayan* style (with the fingers) try **Sinugba.**

Chinese food is the speciality of **White Gold** and **Tung Yan.** Chinese *dim sum* is served at **Ding How Dim Sum.** (For those unfamiliar with *dim sum*, it's sort of a Cantonese automat, where steaming bamboo baskets of delectable dishes are paraded past on carts. Peek under the lids as they pass and order what catches your fancy from among dozens of choices offered.)

Both Japanese and Korean food are the specialities of **The Ginza.**

For continental food, try **Nivel** at the Cebu Plaza Hotel, the **Beehive,** or **Puerto Gallera** at the Magellan Hotel.

Discotheques are the **Disco Pad** at the Magellan Hotel, the **Inner Circle** and the **Altitude.** For sing-along live music, try the **Sigay Bar** at the Magellan Hotel.

Bohol

Bohol's most famous attraction is a unique topographical feature known as the **Chocolate Hills.** Looking at these grass-covered mounds, which number more than a thousand, some 100 metres high, it is easier to accept the local legend of their creation than to believe the scientific explanation. They were formed by the teardrops of an unhappy giant, say the Boholanos. An extremely rare geological process of erosion, say the scientists who come to study them. Whatever their origin, they present a strangely eerie vista, rising from the surrounding plateau like so many jelly drops, green for part of the year and brown during the dry months of summer.

One of the oldest churches in the Philippines stands in a small town seven kilometres from the capital city of Tagbilaran. **Baclayon Church** was built by Jesuits in 1595. Inside, an upstairs storeroom houses a collection of antiques and religious artefacts, some of which predate the church. The caretaker and historian of the church, limited by lack of funds, is doing his

best to preserve this priceless heritage from the onslaught of clever thieves, private collectors and natural deterioration.

Six kilometres from Tagbilaran over good roads is **Hinagdanan Cave,** an underworld cavern with a pool of crystal water lit by two natural skylights. The voices of local youngsters echo back from the stalagmites and stalactites as they dive from high boulders into the depths of the pool.

Pirate raids were a fact of life during Spanish colonial times, as the many ruins of stone watch-towers dotting the coasts of Cebu and Bohol testify. One of the best preserved is **Punta Cross Watch-tower,** 14 kilometres from the capital.

A point within the capital city near Barrio Bool is said to have been the spot where Legazpi and local chieftain Datu Sikatuna sealed a blood pact of friendship. A marker memorialises the event.

The Gie Gardens Hotel on M.H. Del Pilar Street in Tagbilaran City offers adequate accommodation and a restaurant.

Iloilo

The province of Iloilo on the southeastern side of the island of Panay boasts some of the most splendid examples of Spanish colonial churches in the Philippines. It is also noted for its *jusi* and *pina* fabrics, used in making the *barong tagalog,* and for *pancit molo,* a soup which originated there and is now found on menus all over the archipelago.

Iloilo City is the capital of the province. At the mouth of the Iloilo River overlooking the sea is **Fort San Pedro,** an old Spanish fortress. Its ramparts are now a popular spot for strolling in the late afternoon. **Museo Iloilo,** a modern building on Bonifacio Drive, has a fine collection of pre-Spanish artefacts collected from ancient burial sites, among them gold-leaf masks for the dead, ornamented teeth and primitive jewellery. Other exhibits include Stone Age tools, liturgical art, and some of the cargo retrieved from the wreck of a 19th century British ship that sank off nearby Guimaras island.

Molo district was the Parian, or Chinese quarter, in Spanish times. Fronting the large, tree-shaded plaza is **Molo Church,** a Gothic Renaissance structure built of coral rock in the 19th century. On the columns on either side of the central aisle are sixteen large images of saints, all female, giving rise to local residents' humorous references to their Church of Women's Liberation. Also in Molo is **Asilo de Molo,** an orphanage where the children turn out beautifully embroidered church vestments. Visitors are welcome.

In both Molo and Jaro districts handsome old houses of the last century still stand. Although many have been converted into hotels or religious retreats, some are still used as residences. Weavers of *pina* and *jusi* may be observed in the gardens of some of the old homes of Jaro.

Arevalo district was once the political and military capital of Western

Visayas, but was destroyed by the Dutch in 1614. It is now known as the 'Flower Village' for the corsages, wreaths and bouquets produced there.

Just across from Iloilo City, 15 minutes by pump boat, is **Guimaras island,** with lovely beaches, caves and falls.

Twelve kilometres west of Iloilo City is **Anhawan Beach Resort,** offering cottages, a good seafood restaurant and a children's playground. Twenty-eight kilometres further in the same direction is golden sandstone **Miagao Church,** one of the most interesting baroque churches in the province. Its facade is a unique example of Philippine religious arts, featuring relief carvings of coconut and papaya trees. On the left and right of the banana tree, Adam and Eve are depicted in Filipino dress. The original architectural plan specified twin towers flanking the church. The master builder died after completing the first tower and his successor decided to improve upon the design when building the second tower, giving a slightly haphazard look to the finished structure.

Another twelve kilometres further on is **San Joaquin Church,** made of gleaming white coral rocks. Built in 1869, this church also has an unusual facade depicting the Battle of Tetuan in Morocco in 1859. The lively battle is vividly expressed in high-relief sculpture, lance-wielding Spanish soldiers pursuing Moors while St James looks on.

North from Iloilo City are more magnificent old churches: **Pavia Church, Sta. Barbara Church, Cabatuan Church** and the ruins of **Janiuay Church.**

Twenty minutes by pump boat from Estancia on Panay's northeast coast is **Sicogon island,** now a first-class resort with facilities that include a golf course and swimming pools. And one-and-a-half kilometres off Panay's northwest tip lies tiny **Boracay island,** where almost deserted white sand beaches of talcum powder consistency and waters of crystal clarity present an idyllic paradise.

Hotels

Hotel Del Rio, M.H. Del Pilar, Molo District (Tel. 75585).
Iloilo Casa Plaza, Iznart Street (Tel. 73461).
Sarabia Manor, Gen. Luna Street (Tel. 72732).

Bacolod

Across the channel from Panay is Bacolod, capital of western Negros. This is sugar country, and the landscape is characterised by vast stretches of sugarcane plantations. Anaware ceramics of fine quality are produced here, and attractive artificial flowers made from wood shavings. Local delicacies are *inasal,* chicken barbecued with lemon grass, and *La Paz batchoy,* a noodle dish.

A pleasant plaza with lighted fountains and amplified music is at the centre of Bacolod City. Cultural programmes are held here on Sunday

Pavia Church, Iloilo

afternoons. An oasis of tranquil beauty is provided in the **Provincial Capitol Park** surrounding the capitol building.

Just north of Bacolod, in the small town of Silay, several old Spanish houses still stand. The **Holifena Art Collection,** at 21 de Noviembre Street, contains some works of early Filipino masters.

Victorias Milling Co., said to be the largest sugar mill and refinery in the world, is 37 kilometres north of Bacolod. Visitors may witness the process of sugar production, from the milling of newly harvested canes to the rigorously antiseptic final packaging. The compound surrounding the mill and refinery has all the comforts of a small town—market, cinema, golf course and a small airport. It also has the Chapel of St Joseph the Worker, where a colourful mural and mosaic made from pop bottles shows brown-skinned saints in Filipino costume.

The province's greatest attractions are unquestionably the beaches that line its coast. **Llacaon island,** 50 kilometres north of Bacolod, has excellent beaches. Inland resorts are **Sta. Fe Resort,** seven kilometres east of Bacolod, and **Mambucal Summer Resort,** 32 kilometres southeast. Mambucal is especially attractive, located in cool mountain reaches with hot springs, waterfalls and swimming pools fed by natural springs. It has a lodge, cottages and camping grounds.

Kanlaon Volcano, 100 kilometres from Bacolod, is a favourite of

mountain climbers. At the summit, climbers can peer into the depths of its still-active crater.

Hotels

Sugarland Hotel, Singcang, Bacolod City (Tel. 22462).
Sea Breeze, San Juan Street, Bacolod City (Tel. 24571).
Bascon Hotel II, Gonzaga Street, Bacolod City (Tel. 23141; 23161).

Mindanao

Mindanao is the largest southern island of the Philippines. Dangling from its western side, the long finger of the Zamboanga peninsula points towards North Borneo across the Celebes Sea. The small islands of the Sulu archipelago, like so many drops scattered from the tip of the finger, form stepping-stones between the two land masses. Centuries before the present political boundaries were drawn, seafaring people plied these waters, bartering goods, pirating one another's vessels and diffusing cultures. This, plus the force of Islam spreading outwards from Brunei in the 15th century, led to greater similarities with Indonesian culture than with that of the northern Philippines.

The Spaniards never did succeed in bringing the Moros, as they termed the southern Muslims, into the embrace of colonialism. The Americans managed to quell resistance and establish a fragile peace in the region, but trouble erupted again in the early 1970s, triggered mainly by resentment of the influx of settlers from the north. Eventually, armed guerilla groups merged to become the Moro National Liberation Front (MNLF), whose avowed purpose is to establish an autonomous Muslim state under Filipino sovereignty.

The activities of the Muslim autonomists, combined with those of the New People's Army, an anti-government guerilla group with communist leanings, led the government to impose a travel ban on foreigners to areas outside major cities. The ban has now been lifted, but the news has not reached all government troops, and travellers outside well-populated areas may be questioned. At any rate, the tourist bent on visiting remote areas is advised to report in to provincial or city government officials before setting out.

The Muslim population thins out progressively as one moves eastwards on Mindanao, from 90 percent in Lanao del Sur to less than five percent in Davao on the opposite side of the island. In the hinterlands, and largely inaccessible to the average tourist, live some of the most colourful minority ethnic groups of the Philippines. In 1966 a small isolated band of people, the Tasadays, were discovered in the high altitude rain forests of South Cotabato living a virtual Stone Age existence. Other groups have become 'westernised' to the point of adopting Christianity, but still maintain their cultural traditions.

From Zamboanga it is possible to fly on to Jolo and finally Tawi-Tawi, the southernmost part of the Philippines, where foreign visitors are a rarity.

Zamboanga

Zamboanga City is invariably included on any tour of the south. Some theorise that the name derived from the Malay word *jambangan*, meaning 'a place of flowers'. Others insist that it is a corruption of the Malay *sambuan*, meaning 'mooring posts'. Linguistics aside, Zamboanga, lush with orchid gardens, dozens of varieties of bougainvilleas, roadside displays of red and yellow cannas and flowering creepers, deserves its sobriquet City of Flowers. It is also blessed in having no pronounced wet or dry season, and lying outside the typhoon belt.

The picturesque backdrop for the small city is its seafront, where inter-island ferries, refrigerator boats, fishing vessels known as *basligs*, and little double-rigged *vintas* pass to and fro. And while rapturous descriptions of sunsets tend to glaze the eyes of readers, it's worth noting that sitting at the **Lantaka Hotel's Talisay Bar** (built around the trunk of an ancient tree on the seawall), watching the silhouettes of mooring posts, riggings and masts grow darker against a technicolor background of shifting reds, golds and violets, can be pretty memorable.

At this same seawall behind the Lantaka Hotel, Samal *vintas* tie up to offer displays of sea shells, red and white corals and occasionally turtle shells. Brown-skinned children, their hair bleached blonde by salt water, use all their winsome charms to wheedle passers-by into buying their wares. Some of the children are Bajaus, or sea gypsies, who were born aboard their small vessels and will spend their entire lives on these waterborne homes. Aside from scouring the depths of the sea for its saleable bounty, the Bajaus are also reputed to make the finest double-woven *pandan* mats in the Philippines, which they fan out along the seawall to attract buyers, enlivening the grey stone with geometric patterns of purple, green and gold.

Further along the waterfront, just beyond the market area, Justice R.T. Lim Boulevard, better known by its former name **Cawa Cawa Boulevard,** runs along the sea for two kilometres. It provides a scenic promenade for seashore strollers who don't like sand in their shoes. The boulevard is often likened to a miniature version of Manila's Roxas Boulevard.

The **central plaza** of the city is named after American governor and World War I hero General 'Black Jack' Pershing. A short walk in the direction of the wharf will bring you through Rizal Park (a tiny oasis in the traffic) to **City Hall,** an attractive 1907 building. Zamboanga's idiosyncratic mayor has posted a large 'scoreboard' on the front of City Hall giving

Mosque in Zamboanga

regularly updated figures on persons kidnapped or murdered in the past year. The numbers are impressive, maybe even alarming, considering the size of the city. The mayor's intention is to prick the conscience of the government's peacekeepers, but would seem to operate in direct opposition to the aims of the Ministry of Tourism.

The **Barter Trade Market** was established by the government in an attempt to regulate the influx of untaxed goods from Borneo. The unauthorised trade was viewed by its practitioners as a traditional way of life; the government, taking a different viewpoint, called it smuggling. The Barter Trade Market on the wharf flourished until it burned to the ground in 1979. It was re-established on the outskirts of the city, but met with the same fate as the original market. (Arson, they say.) It is now located near the wharf, but the government has recently suspended the free trade arrangement. Unless the suspension is rescinded, the market's present stock of cassette recorders, cheap mechanical toys, batiks and canned goods, once exhausted, will be its last.

Things to See and Do

Fort Pilar is Zamboanga's major landmark. Built in 1635 by the Spaniards to repel attacks from the Moros, Dutch, Portuguese and British, and then abandoned, it was rebuilt in 1719 and dedicated to Our Lady of

Coral vendor

Pilar. Its one-metre-thick coral stone walls have subsequently housed American troops (in 1898, when it was renamed Pettit Barracks), and the occupying Japanese during World War II. At present it houses not soldiers, but families. When rival factions of smugglers vented their hostilities by setting fire to one another's houses, the mayor kindly gave the homeless families temporary residence inside the fort. Temporary became permanent, and today lines of wash fly in place of flags inside the venerable fortress.

At the eastern entrance to the fort is an open-air shrine to Our Lady of Pilar built to honour the patron saint of Zamboanga. She is credited with many miracles, including sparing the city from the catastrophic tsunamis which struck southern Mindanao in 1976 in the wake of an earthquake, drowning thousands. Those of lesser faith attribute the miracle to the fact that the brunt of the waves was taken by tiny Basilan island, 15 kilometres across the strait, where entire villages were swept away.

Rio Hondo is a picturesque water village of small houses built out over the water on stilts. Located just east of Fort Pilar, it houses Tausugs, Samals and Bajaus who have been coaxed ashore by the government.

Taluksangay Village is situated along the east coast, 16 kilometres from the city. Its countryside setting lends a peaceful, quiet air to this 'stilt village'. Naked little boys moving between sea and shore with the ease of otters make eager subjects for camera-toting visitors. An equally compelling subject for the photographer is the red-domed white mosque, its glittering image reflected in the waters of a blue lagoon. Taluksangay's people engage in fishing and gathering firewood, the latter a practice that is rapidly denuding the mangrove swamps. Interspersed with the piles of firewood along the road leading to the village are mats covered with seaweed spread to dry in the sun.

The **Yakan Weaving Village** houses a few families of Yakans, land dwellers whose native home is Basilan island, south of Zamboanga. Seated on the floors of their small huts, they can be seen patiently handweaving the colourful cloth for which they are famous. You may even see a turbaned old man sitting cross-legged in front of his homemade xylophone-like instrument, lost in the hypnotic tones of his own music.

Pasonanca Park offers cool breezes and greenery unspoiled by landscaping. It boasts three swimming pools fed by river water, a boy scout park and a honeymoon cottage in a tree. Nestled in the branches of a huge acacia tree and reached by a spiral staircase, the **Pasonanca Park Tree House** is the rustic equivalent of a New York studio apartment—beds, kitchen, dining room and bath all snugly fitted into one room. It has a refrigerator, stove and even a telephone. Honeymooners (and those who feel like honeymooners) can enjoy free accommodation for one or two nights by contacting the mayor's office in the City Hall.

Abong-Abong is a large tract of hills and glades being developed as a tourist spot for Zamboanga's residents. Within its boundaries are a swimming hole in a river, the Tomb of the Unknown Soldier, scout camps, and its most ambitious project—the Stations of the Cross built into the side of a hill. This latter attraction is best viewed from a distance, as the road up the hill is suitable for travel only by Jeep or, as the mayor often does on Sundays, by motorcycle.

Twenty kilometres from the city is the **San Ramon Prison and Penal Farm** where woodcarvings produced by the prisoners can be purchased. In this enlightened institution, inmates who qualify are permitted to build nipa huts inside the colony and bring their families to join them.

Don't leave Zamboanga without taking the 15-minute pump boat trip across to **Great Santa Cruz island** where the sugary sand is tinted pink by red coral washed up from the sea. The beach is kept scrupulously clean with daily rakings. There are trees for shade, covered picnic tables and changing rooms, but no fresh water or food available. Bring your own provisions. Snorkelling is excellent in the underwater garden of corals and tropical reef fish surrounding the island. Canvas shoes or plastic slippers should be worn by swimmers, as the sandy beach quickly turns to rocks and corals. An old Bajau cemetery is set back from the shoreline. The graves are topped by wooden markers called *sundoks*. Some take the form of outrigger canoes; others, standing upright, have a roughly human shape.

Graves shaded by a white cloth tied to four pegs signify the resting place of an imam, a Muslim spiritual leader. A fishing village and a pretty lagoon are other attractions of the island.

There are several beaches in the vicinity of the city: **Arcillas Beach Resort** (8.5 kms), **Caragasan Beach** (12 kms), **Talisayan Beach** (20 kms) and **San Ramón Beach** near the penal colony (22 kms). None matches the beauty of Santa Cruz's beach. Facilities are either minimal or non-existent. Visitors to the beach at **Bolong,** 33 kilometres east of the city, can rent rooms by the day, including meals, at the Edward Ilagan residence. Bolong also has a fish market, best seen on Sunday, the village's market day.

The ferry trip to the island province of **Basilan** takes about two hours. This is the home of the Yakans, who still dress in their unisex trousers, fitted tightly from knee to ankle. There is also a Samal water village on the island that can be toured by boat. Basilan is the leading grower of rubber trees in the Philippines, and has the only rubber processing plant in the country.

Golfers may rent equipment at the Zamboanga Golf Course, built by the Americans and said to be the oldest 18-hole course in the country.

The Zamboanga Plaza Hotel has a lawn tennis court and there are clay and cement courts at the Cabato Lawn Tennis Courts and the Zamboanga Lawn Tennis Association.

Shopping

The Sulu Sea is one of the richest sources of **sea shells** in the world. The serious collector will find bargains in rare specimens here, while the not-so-serious collector can walk off with a suitcase full of pretty shells for a few dollars. On San Jose Road in the direction of the Yakan Weaving Village there are a number of shell shops. Among them are the Rocan Shell Shop, San Luis Shell Factory and Profeta Marine Products. Ertan Specimen Shell is located on Dr Evangelista Road.

Native products can be purchased at Zamboanga Home Products in the Zamboanga Hotel building at Etnika, across the street and up a bit from the Lantaka Hotel, and at G.Q. Native Products on San Jose Road, among others. Along Row C, behind the meat and fish sections of the public market, are a number of stalls selling a similar variety of goods. Be prepared to do some hard bargaining here, as the initial asking price may be double what you will eventually have to pay. There are **wood products** with mother-of-pearl inlays, **woven materials** made into bags, table runners and place-mats, and lengths of material used as *malongs,* the tubular wrap-around garment worn by the Muslim women. The famous wavy-bladed ***kris,*** with its ornately carved handle, and miniature cannons known as ***lantakas,*** make interesting souvenirs. The urn-shaped ***kabul,*** its intricate designs either hand-engraved on brass or painstakingly fashioned with copper wire, is an especially beautiful decorative item.

Fishermen dragging in their nets

Sulu pearls and **semi-precious stones** wrapped in grubby paper routinely emerge from the pockets of shabbily dressed entrepreneurs who hang about the tourist spots. Good buys can be made by those who know their jewels and are determined bargainers.

Restaurants and Nightlife

Alavar's House of Seafoods on Cawa Cawa Avenue is a good place to have Zamboanga's speciality, the *curacha*. This odd-looking crab, red even before cooking, is quite delicious served with Alavar's special coconut-based sauce. Their *bagoong* (fermented shrimp sauce), also prepared with coconut milk, eaten as a dip with slices of green mango, is another speciality to be sampled. Seafood dishes star at the **Kamayan Restaurant** of the Zamboanga Plaza Hotel as well.

The **Aristocrat Luncheonette** on G. Nacional serves Chinese food, as does **City Lunch** on Gov. Lim Avenue. For Filipino dishes, try the **Bulakena** on Tetuan Highway or, at lunchtime, the newly-built open-air restaurant just outside the entrance of **Pasonanca Park,** constructed to simulate a passenger train.

For nightlife, try the casino or the **Cobweb Discotheque** at the Zamboanga Plaza Hotel. There are the usual number of girlie bars and strip joints scattered around the city, although cynical residents claim the girls attached to these establishments are 'Cebu's rejects'.

Hotels

The **Zamboanga Plaza Hotel** on the outskirts of the city is a luxury-class hotel. It has a swimming pool, tennis court, good restaurants and bar, an adjacent casino and the cool breezes of an elevated location.

The **Lantaka Hotel** (full name Lantaka-by-the-Sea) is not luxury class, but it's comfortable and has the advantage of being within walking distance of most of the city's attractions. It also has a swimming pool and a seafront location.

Davao

The Philippines' third largest city, Davao, tucked up inside the embrace of the Davao Gulf, is the home town of the durian, that delicious fruit whose unfortunate lingering odour is so powerful that it is barred from the cabins of Philippine Airlines flights. The juiciest pomelos, the sweetest lanzones and the creamiest atis—all tropical fruits of paradise—also come from here. Davao is the centre of Mindanao's logging, mining and agricultural industries as well.

Visits to nearby ***ramie, abaca*** **and banana plantations** and to plywood factories can usually be arranged through hotels. Also open to visitors is **Nenita Stock Farm** (known locally as Pork's Park, after the similarly named

Muslim women of Mindanao

Forbes Park, Manila's ghetto for the wealthy), a huge piggery where the stock enjoy the kind of pampering their barrio cousins can only dream of.

The city itself has little of interest, but the **Lon Wa Temple** on Leon Garcia Street, serving the very large Chinese population of the city, is the biggest temple on Mindanao and worth a visit for its representative Chinese arts and architecture. There is also a small Muslim stilt village within the city, located near **Magsaysay Park** on Quezon Boulevard.

Several good black sand beaches—**Guiono-o, Salokot, Talisay** and **Talomo**—are accessible from the city by taxi or jeepney. The number one 'must do' activity for outdoorsmen in Davao is the trek up nearby **Mount Apo,** highest mountain in the country. The climb is long, but not difficult, and takes anywhere from two to four days depending on your fitness and vitality. Mt Apo is a volcano, and climbers who reach the top can take back pieces of its yellow, sulphurous crater rocks as souvenirs. (See page 72 for details of the climb.)

About four kilometres southeast of Davao City is the **Shrine of the Holy Infant Jesus of Prague.** This holy place, so goes the story, grew from a miraculous religious experience. The wife of the city mayor was prompted by a vision to go to Czechoslovakia and bring back a replica of the Holy Infant Jesus and build a shrine in its honour. Since then another replica of Jesus from Fatima, Portugal has been similarly enshrined and a whole complex of chapels, altars, statues and seminar halls have sprung up.

Eleven kilometres from the city is the **Apo Golf and Country Club,** with a very good 18-hole golf course. Just off the same main road on the right is **Caroland Resort.** Swimming, boating, fishing and horseback riding are offered here. A special added attraction is a pond stocked with fat carp. Visitors hold bread between their teeth, lean over and wait for a clever fish to swim by and snatch it.

The island of **Samal** is a one-hour trip across the gulf. Pump boats may be rented at Santa Ana pier, or you may go on an organised tour. There is a Muslim settlement, **San Jose Village,** on the island. En route is **Aguinaldo Pearl Farm,** which sounds much more interesting than it is. It is now no more than a small resort with a hotel and a pleasant beach.

Another Muslim village can be seen at **Wangan, Calinan.** The people here are Bagobos, a rapidly diminishing tribe known for their woven *abaca* cloth and distinctive attire. Arrangements must be made in advance in order to see them in traditional dress, as they now don their tribal costumes only on special occasions.

Shops, Hotels and Restaurants

All the ethnic handicrafts of the south are available in the shops of Aldevinco Shopping Centre off Claro M. Recto Avenue, the largest in the city. There are baskets, brassware, batiks, weaving and musical instruments, to name but a few.

The **Davao Insular Inter-Continental** is a fine hotel, considered a destination resort by Filipinos and foreigners alike. Other good hotels are the **Apo View** on J. Camus Street and the **Hotel Maguindanao** at 86 Clara M. Recto Avenue.

The Davao Insular Inter-Continental Inn has several restaurants: The **Mandaya Room,** serving both native and continental cuisine; **La Parilla,** which specialises in grilled seafoods; a coffee shop; and the **Vinta Bar.** The hotel also has a casino.

Apo View Hotel has a Japanese restaurant, the **Mikado,** a bar and a discotheque.

The Maguindanao Hotel has a Chinese restaurant, the **Yangtse,** and a newly-opened restaurant, **Socorro's,** the only one in the city specialising in Spanish cuisine.

In the city the **Harana, Hongkong Restaurant** and **Davao Inihaw** enjoy a good reputation. Bands and combos play in Davao's larger hotels and in the numerous discos and supper clubs throughout the city.

Cagayan de Oro and Beyond

Cagayan de Oro is the gateway to northern Mindanao. It is a progressive city, with modern hotels and restaurants, government and office buildings and a large university. The **Xavier University Folk Museum** is small, but has an interesting array of tribal artefacts and archaeological findings.

Seven kilometres from the city is the **Del Monte pineapple canning plant,** which offers guided tours. It is also possible to visit Philippine Packing Corporation's huge pineapple plantation about 30 kilometres from Cagayan de Oro. The plantation has its own landing strip and golf course.

Opol Beach, fronting a fishing village known for its fresh fish and shrimps, is the best of the nearby beaches. Another place to swim, and a pleasant nature spot as well, is small but lovely **Catanico Falls,** which cascades between large boulders to a natural pool below. The falls are 20 minutes by car from the city centre.

If you're fascinated by caves, there are some good opportunities to explore in this area. Fourteen kilometres from the city, situated in a rugged ravine overlooking the Cagayan River, is **Macahambus Cave,** a big one. More difficult to reach, but interesting as the site of diggings which produced Neolithic Age artefacts, are the **Huluga Caves.** Getting to the three small caves involves walking through fields and hauling oneself up a high embankment through the tangled branches of an enormous tree that seems to have become one with the hill.

The larger hotels—**Hotel Mindanao** and **Alta Tierra**—have airconditioned rooms and restaurants. The Ministry of Tourism located in the Marcos Sports Centre complex maintains a list of recommended hotels

and restaurants and current tariffs. The usual city transport—jeepneys and PUs—are available, plus the *motorela*, a motorcyle hitched to a six-passenger chassis.

Cagayan de Oro serves as a jumping-off point to some of the Philippines' less frequently visited, but delightful, attractions.

A short flight by Aerotransport will bring you to **Camiguin,** also known as Hibok-Hibok island, after the small, deadly volcano by the same name. In a 1951 eruption, red-hot volcanic material swept down the slopes with hurricane speed, claiming more than 600 lives. Actually, Hibok-Hibok is only one of seven volcanoes sharing space on tiny Camiguin. The island has a government volcanology station which may be visited. A circumferential road runs round the island, passing some of the most beautiful white sand beaches in the Philippines, as well as the former capital, Bonbon, which met with disaster in a volcanic eruption more than a hundred years ago. (A sunken cemetery, tombstones still standing, is said to lie beneath the sea at this point.) Cascading waterfalls, lagoons and hot springs make Camiguin's interior a paradise of unspoiled beauty.

Heading in the opposite direction from Cagayan de Oro, a two-hour drive takes one through **Iligan City** and on to **Maria Cristina Falls,** the tallest and most beautiful in the country. There is a hydroelectric plant at the falls, with an observation platform.

One hour beyond Iligan City is **Marawi** and volcanic **Lake Lanao,** where fine Maranao brassware is produced. The dress of the women here is a visual delight; vibrant-toned *malongs* and fancy jewellery are their everyday garb. Islam is practised with a fierce devotion in this area, its influence clearly seen in the sinuous *okir* art forms and the ornately carved roofs of the *torrogan*, communal houses of the sultans. There are several mosques, the newest being the **King Faisal Mosque** on the grounds of **Mindanao State University.** The **Aga Khan Museum** houses a rich collection of Maranao ethnic arts and crafts. Handicrafts that look as though they came from the museum can be purchased in the **Politan,** or marketplace, where small makeshift shops feature a dizzying display of goods—brass gongs, betel boxes, bells, mats, handwoven fabrics and bamboo tobacco containers decorated in the favourite purple, green and yellow *okir* design of the region.

A marker in Marawi City indicates Zero Point, from which all points on Mindanao are measured.

Palawan

Palawan is the name given to both the province and main island of the Philippines' westernmost territory. One quarter of the archipelago's 7,000 islands are contained in this province, their crystal waters and white sand beaches providing ideal opportunities for swimming, diving and fishing. Fully 65 percent the country's fish supply comes from Palawan.

The main island, the Philippines' fifth largest, is rich in timber and minerals. Its relative isolation from the rest of the country has left it largely unexplored and undeveloped, but an oil strike off its shores in 1976 generated new interest. Its capital, Puerto Princesa, now boasts a five-star hotel, the Hyatt Rafols. Just beyond the outskirts of the small town, however, roads degenerate into rugged paths traversable only by Jeep or bus. For this reason, the primitive delights of the island are recommended only for hardy and adventurous travellers.

Palawan is known as the cradle of Philippine civilisation after the discovery of the Tabon Man skull and other paleolithic artefacts said to predate the Australian aborigines. The site of the discovery, the **Tabon Caves,** is a huge complex of caves of which only a small part has been explored. Archaeological digging is still going on. The entrance to the main cave is high up on a promontory overlooking a beautiful bay and beach. Reaching the caves requires a rough five-hour jeepney ride overland, followed by a 30-minute pump boat ride.

After Tabon Caves, Palawan's most famous attraction is **St Paul's Subterranean River,** which winds underground for five kilometres and empties into the South China Sea. A two-hour jeepney trip plus another two hours by pump boat brings you to the mouth of the river. Visitors can travel along the river in a small boat and admire the glittering stalactites and awesome marble-domed passage by the light of carbide lamps.

Twenty-five kilometres south of Puerto Princesa is the **Iwahig Penal Colony,** a prison without bars. Inmates here farm the land and produce and sell wood and mother-of-pearl inlaid handicrafts. There is also a mini zoo of Palawan's exotic fauna, some of which are unique only to this island.

It is possible to visit the **Batak,** one of the most primitive cultural minorities of the Philippines, by travelling one hour from Puerto Princesa by jeepney and then hiking an additional one hour and twenty minutes. The Batak women go topless and the men wear only G-strings. They are a hunting, food-gathering tribe who use expertly aimed blowguns with feathered darts to bring down their game.

The entire province of Palawan has been declared a game refuge and bird sanctuary. **Ursula island,** off the southeastern coast, provides a breathtaking spectacle each evening at sunset when hundreds of thousands of birds come home from the mainland to roost. And at the northern tip of the island is **El Nido** ('the Nest') where fishing villages nestle against blue-black marble cliffs rising out of the sea. The cliffs are home to the tiny swifts whose nests are gathered and sold in Manila for the Chinese delicacy bird's nest soup.

The Hyatt Rafols is a five-star hotel in Puerto Princesa City. It has restaurants, a swimming pool, golf course and tennis court.

The Penafrancia fluvial parade

Recommended Reading

The Ministry of Tourism at Agrifina Circle, Rizal Park in Manila has many useful publications on the Philippines for tourists.

There are two publications, usually available in hotel bookshops, that are particularly useful to the traveller who likes to chart his own voyage of discovery. *The Metro Manila Street Guide,* published by Raya Books, Hong Kong, has detailed maps of Metro Manila and an easy-to-use index of streets, public buildings, landmarks, etc. If you intend to drive farther afield from Manila, the *Caltex Philippines Travel Guide,* published by National Book Store, has maps, foolproof directions, and estimated travel times to popular destinations. Of special interest to divers is *The Divers' Guide to the Philippines,* by David Smith and Michael Westlake.

A useful little handbook for those bent on exploring Manila's exotic and erotic nightlife is *Manila By Night,* by CFW Guidebooks, Hong Kong, also available in Manila.

For a brief, painless overview of Philippine history, read *Dioramas,* published by, and available at, the Ayala Museum in Manila. A fluid account of the country's development is illustrated with the museum's own excellent dioramas.

National hero Jose Rizal's two famous books that once inflamed a nation are *Noli Me Tangere* and *El Filibusterismo*. Philippine Education Company, Manila publishes English translations called *The Social Cancer* and *The Reign of Greed* respectively.

Jeepney, by Emmanuel Torres, is a colourful little book that tells you all you want to know, in photographs and text, about that brash and gaudy vehicle.

If you would like to know more about the carvings, weaving, brassware and other ethnic arts of the minorities, *The People and Art of the Philippines*, published by the Museum of Cultural History, University of California, is available in some Manila bookshops.

Faith Healing and Psychic Surgery, by Lava and Araneta, is a personal account of their journey into that strange world by two respected writers.

Pearls and Coconuts, by Frances H. Engel, presents history, customs and personal observations from the viewpoint of a long-time American resident of the Philippines.

Coffee table books on Philippine culture, beautifully illustrated, are *The Culinary Culture of the Philippines*, by Gilda Cordero-Fernando, and *Fiesta*, by Alejandro R. Roces. On a smaller scale, an excellent photographic overview of the country is provided in *Philippines in Focus*, with photography by Alain Evrard and text by Simon Barnes.

And if you really want to become an expert on Philippine culture and history, *Filipino Heritage*, published by Lahing Pilipino Publishing Inc., is a ten-volume series of information, encyclopaedic in coverage, but fascinating in presentation. The volumes may be purchased separately.

Appendix

Airline Offices

Air France—Manila Hilton, UN Ave., Ermita (Tel. 5217501).
British Airways—Legazpi corner De La Rose St., Makati (Tel. 8170361).
Cathay Pacific Airways—Ermita Centre Bldg, Roxas Blvd (Tel. 598061).
China Airlines—Manila Hilton, UN Ave., Ermita (Tel. 599460).
Japan Air Lines—Bayview Prince Hotel, Roxas Blvd (Tel. 505611).
Korean Air Lines—Bayview Prince Hotel, Roxas Blvd. (Tel. 5220526).
KLM—Atheneum Bldg, Avaro St., Makati (Tel. 8159701).
Northwest Orient Airlines—1020 Roxas Blvd (Tel. 5211911)
Philippine Airlines—(1) Central Bank Bldg, Roxas Blvd (Tel. 507878); and (2) Inter-Continental Hotel, Makati (Tel. 893654).
Qantas Airways—China Bank Bldg, Pasco de Roxas, Makati (Tel. 8159491).
SAS—Oledan Bldg, 131 Ayala Ave., Makati (Tel. 8872118).
Singapore Airlines—138 H.V. de la Costa, Makati (Tel. 8188341).
Swissair—Country Space 1 Bldg, Sen Gil Puyat Ave., Makati (Tel. 8188351)
Thai International—Manila Hilton Hotel, UN Ave., Ermita (Tel. 573711).
United Airlines—ALPAP Bldg, 140 Alfaro St., Sakedo Vill, Makati (Tel. 8185421).

Churches

Information about English-language services in Manila may be obtained by calling the following representative of major denominations:

Baptist—Bible Baptist Church, 23 ROTC Hunters Ave., Fatalon (Tel: 7112888).
Catholic—Manila Cathedral, Aduana Street and Calle Real, Intramuros (Tel. 481243).
Episcopal—Church of the Holy Trinity, 48 McKinley Road, Makati (Tel. 8179440).
Jewish—Jewish Association of the Philippines, Tordisillas St, Makati.
Methodist—Central United Methodist Church, 594 TM Kalaw (Tel: 571491).
Lutheran—Lutheran Church in the Philippines, 4461 Old Santa Mesa (Tel. 605041).
Islam—Metro Manila golden Mosque, Globo de Oro, Quiapo.

In addition, inter-denominational Christian services are held for the English-speaking international community at Union Church of Manila, Legaspi Village, Makati at 8.30 am and 10 am on Sundays (Tel. 889981).

Embassies

Australia—Bank of Pil Island Bldg, Paseo de Roxas, Makati (Tel. 8177911).
Austria—Prince Bldg, 117 Rada St, Legaspi Village (Tel. 8179191).

Belgium—Don Jacinto Bldg, Legaspi Village (Tel. 876571).
Canada—Allied Bank Bldg, 6754 Ayala Ave. (Tel. 8159536 to 41).
China—4896 Pasay Rd, Dasmarinas Vill (Tel. 853148).
Denmark—Citibank Centre, 8741 Paseo de Roxas (Tel. 876556).
France—Fil Life Assurance Bldg, 6786 Ayala St (Tel. 876561).
Germany—Citibank Centre, 8741 Paseo de Roxas (Tel. 864906).
India—2190 Paraiso, Makati (Tel. 872445).
Indonesia—Salcedo St, Legaspi village (Tel. 855061).
Israel—Phil Saving Bldg, 6813 Ayala Ave., (Tel. 885329).
Italy—191 Salcedo St, Legaspi Village (Tel. 874531).
Japan—L.C. Bldg, 375 Sen. Gil Puyat Ave. (Tel. 8189010).
Korea—140 Alvarado St, Salcedo Village (Tel. 8175705).
Malaysia—Republic Glass Bldg, Tordecillas St. (Tel. 8174581).
Mexico—814 Pasay Rd, Makati (Tel. 857323).
New Zealand—Gammon Centre Bldg, 126 Alfaro St., Salcedo Vill (Tel. 8180910).
Norway—Corner Salcedo & Herrera, Legaspi Village (Tel. 881111).
Pakistan—Cibeles Bldg, 6780 Ayala Ave. (Tel. 8172776).
Singapore—217 Salcedo St, Legaspi Village, Makati (Tel. 8161764).
Spain—Corner Salcedo & Herrera, Legaspi Village (Tel. 8183561).
Sweden—Citibank Centre, 8741 Paseo de Roxas, Makati (Tel. 858746).
Switzerland—140 Amorsolo, Makati (Tel. 8190202).
Thailand—San Miguel Bldg, Ayala Ave. (Tel. 888961).
United Kingdom—115 Esteban St, Legaspi Village (Tel. 853002 to 09)
United States of America—1210 Roxas Blvd (Tel. 5217116).

Ministry of Tourism Offices

Main Office—Ground Floor, Tourism Bldg, Agrifina Circle, Rizal Park, Manila (Tel. 599031)
Field Offices:
Angeles City—Dau Interchange, Mabalacat, Pampanga (Tel. 6292243).
Baguio City—MOT Complex, Gov. Pack Road (Tel. 5015, 5416, 6858, 4906).
Bacolod City—Villasor Bldg, Luzurriaga St (Tel. 27662).
Cagayan de Oro City—Marcos Sports Centre complex (Tel. 3340).
Cebu City—Fort San Pedro (Tel. 91503).
Davao City—Apo View Hotel, J. Camus St (Tel. 74861).
Iloilo City—Sarabia Bldg, Gen. Luna St (Tel. 78701).
La Union—Cresta del Mar Beach Resort, Paringao, Bauang, La Union (Tel. 412411).
Legazpi City—Penaranda Park, Albay District (Tel. 4492).
Marawi City—Ford Guest House No.2, Mindanao State University (Tel. 589255).
Tacloban City—Children's Park, Sen. Enage St (Tel. 2048).
Zamboanga City—Lantaka Hotel, Valderosa St (Tel. 3931).

Index

D

E

F

T

U

V

W

Y

Z